About the Authors

Alex de Waal is a writer and activist on African issues. He is a fellow of the Global Equity Initiative, Harvard; director of the Social Science Research Council program on AIDS and social transformation; and a director of Justice Africa in London. In his twenty-year career he has studied the social, political and health dimensions of famine, war, genocide and the HIV/AIDS epidemic, especially in the Horn of Africa and the Great Lakes. He has been at the forefront of mobilizing African and international responses to these problems. His books include *Famine that Kills: Darfur Sudan* (Oxford University Press, 1st edn 1989, revised 2004), *Famine Crimes: Politics and the Disaster Relief Industry in Africa* (James Currey, 1997) and *Islamism and Its Enemies in the Horn of Africa* (Hurst, 2004).

Julie Flint is a journalist and film-maker who divides her time between London and the Middle East. In a thirty-year career she has worked on four continents, from Colombia to China, and won awards for newspapers, radio and television. She has been writing about Sudan since 1992, initially for the *Guardian* and later as a freelance with a special interest in human rights. She has written extensively on the Nuba of Sudan, the oil war in southern Sudan and, most recently, Darfur. Her work includes *Sudan's Secret War* (BBC 2, 1995), *The Scorched Earth* (Christian Aid, 2001) and *Darfur Destroyed* (Human Rights Watch, 2004).

Darfur

A Short History of a Long War

Julie Flint and Alex de Waal

ZED BOOKS
London & New York

DAVID PHILIP
Cape Town

in association with

INTERNATIONAL AFRICAN INSTITUTE

To Hussein Dafa'alla, 12, who escaped with his life,
and the countless others who didn't

Darfur: A Short History of a Long War was first published in 2005 by

In Southern Africa: David Philip (an imprint of New Africa Books),
99 Garfield Road, Claremont 7700, South Africa

In the rest of the world by Zed Books Ltd, 7 Cynthia Street, London N1 9JF,
UK, and Room 400, 175 Fifth Avenue, New York, NY 10010, USA

www.zedbooks.co.uk

Picture credits: pp. 2, 4, 6, 34, 44, 47 Alex de Waal;
pp. 67, 74, 114, 133 Julie Flint; pp. 110, 111 Darfur
Centre for Human Rights and Development.

Designed and typeset in Monotype Joanna
by illuminati, Grosmont, www.illuminatibooks.co.uk
Cover designed by Andrew Corbett
Printed and bound by Cox & Wyman, Reading

Distributed in the USA exclusively by Palgrave Macmillan, a division of
St Martin's Press, LLC, 175 Fifth Avenue, New York, NY 10010

A catalogue record for this book is available from the British Library
Library of Congress Cataloging-in-Publication Data available

ISBN 1 84277 696 7 Hb
ISBN 1 84277 697 5 Pb

AFRICAN ARGUMENTS

*A new series from Zed Books
in association with the International African Institute*

African Arguments is a series of short books about Africa today. Aimed at the growing number of students and general readers who want to know more about the continent, these books intend to highlight many of the longer-term strategic as well immediate political issues confronting the African continent. They will get to the heart of why Africa is the way it is and how it is changing. The books are scholarly but engaged, substantive as well as topical.

Series editors

ALEX DE WAAL, Global Equity Initiative, Harvard University
RICHARD DOWDEN, Executive Director, Royal African Society
TAJUDEEN ABDUL-RAHEEM, Director, Justice Africa

Editorial board

ABDUl MOHAMMED, InterAfrica Group
EMMANUEL AKYEAMPONG, Professor of History, Harvard University
TIM ALLEN, London School of Economics
ALCINDA HONWANA, Social Science Research Council, New York

Titles in preparation

Tim Allen, *Trial Justice: The International Criminal Court and the Lord's Resistance Army*
Alex de Waal, *AIDS and Power: Democracy, Activism and Disease in Africa*
Tajudeen Abdul Raheem, *The African Union: Fresh Start in Africa?*
Richard Dowden and Simon Maxwell, *Aid to Africa: Solution or Millstone?*

African Arguments is published by Zed Books and the IAI
with the support of the following organizations:

Global Equity Initiative   The Global Equity Initiative seeks to advance
the understanding and tackle the challenges of global inequitable
development. Located at Harvard University, it has international
collaborative research programmes on security, health, capabilities
and philanthropy.

InterAfrica Group   The InterAfrica Group is the regional centre for
dialogue on issues of development, democracy, conflict resolution and
humanitarianism in the Horn of Africa. It was founded in 1988 and
is based in Addis Ababa; it has programmes supporting democracy
in Ethiopia and partnership with the African Union and IGAD.

International African Institute   The International African Institute's
principal aim is to promote scholarly understanding of Africa, notably
its changing societies, cultures and languages. Founded in 1926 and
based in London, it supports a range of seminars and publications
including the journal *Africa*.

Justice Africa   Justice Africa initiates and supports African civil society
activities in support of peace, justice and democracy in Africa. Founded
in 1999, it has a range of activities supporting peace in the Horn of
Africa, HIV/AIDS and democracy, and the African Union.

Royal African Society   Now more than a hundred years old, the
Royal African Society is today Britain's leading organization promoting
Africa's cause. Through its journal, *African Affairs*, and by organizing
meetings, discussions and other activities, the Society strengthens
links between Africa and Britain and encourages understanding of
Africa and its relations with the rest of the world.

Social Science Research Council   The Social Science Research Council
brings necessary knowledge to public issues. Founded in 1923 and
based in New York, it brings together researchers, practitioners and
policymakers on every continent.

Contents

Acknowledgements

This book was possible because of the extensive cooperation and sharing of insights by a large number of people from Darfur and elsewhere in Sudan. Many of these must remain unnamed, at least for now. Hafiz Ismail and Sid Ahmed Bilal translated documents and interviews. Airserv provided hospitality and many small kindnesses in Chad. The project was funded by a grant from the Ford Foundation to Justice Africa.

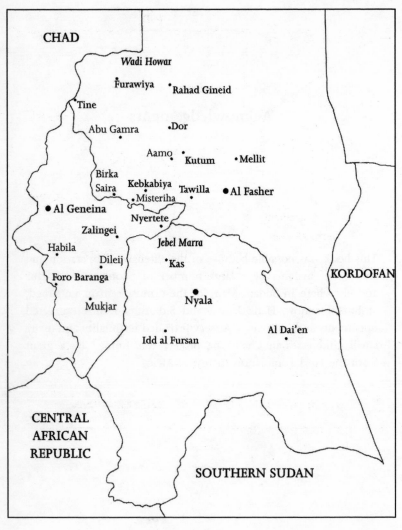

Darfur

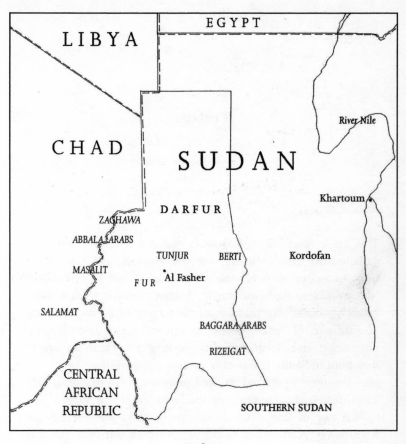

Sudan

Preface

This book describes and analyses the storm clouds that have gathered over Darfur in the last twenty years, and that finally burst in an explosion of violence that the United Nations called 'the world's worst humanitarian disaster' and the United States called 'genocide'. For many years the tragedy of Darfur, a wholly Muslim part of Sudan, developed unseen, screened off by the government and overshadowed by the long civil war in the largely non-Muslim South. It was only in 2004, as government violence plumbed new depths and terrified survivors began straggling into Chad, that Darfur became impossible to ignore any longer.

The war in Darfur has been compared to the genocide in Rwanda ten years earlier, to the North–South war in Sudan that was settled just as Darfur erupted, and even to the conflict in Iraq. In *Darfur: A Short History of a Long War*, we seek to tell Darfur's story in its own terms. We trace the local, national and regional origins of the disaster, drawing on research we have undertaken, separately and jointly, in Darfur since 1985.

This book goes to press at a historic moment for Sudan. On 31 July, John Garang, commander-in-chief of the Sudan People's Liberation Army and for just three weeks First Vice President in a new Government of National Unity, died in a helicopter crash.

In the blink of an eye, the 'Comprehensive Peace Agreement' (CPA) lost the man who consummated three years of painstaking negotiations when he signed it in Nairobi on 9 January 2005. The agreement, drafted on a simplified North–South dichotomy, does not satisfy Darfur's demands and the rebels insist that its power-sharing provisions must be renegotiated. But Garang's presence in the Khartoum government would have been a powerful force against government-sponsored aggression in Darfur. An uncompromising advocate of ethnic and religious equality across the country, he was the guarantor of the peace in the South and, by extension, in the wider Sudan.

Although it resolves just one of Sudan's many conflicts, the CPA, now imperilled, is a tremendous achievement, regarded as an impossible dream only a few years ago. For Darfur, however, it holds out peril along with promise. The men who head the new government know that their credibility and future political and financial support depend upon ending Darfur's agony. But the CPA is a deal between northern and southern military elites that short-changes Darfur's share of the nation's power and resources.

Just three days before Garang flew to Khartoum for his swearing-in ceremony, peace talks on Darfur mediated by the African Union achieved a rare breakthrough. The Sudan government and the two Darfurian rebel fronts – the Sudan Liberation Army and the Justice and Equality Movement – signed a 'Declaration of Principles' that provides a political framework for peace and reflects a new realism on all sides. It was a success for the AU's new chief mediator, Salim Ahmed Salim. A former secretary general of the Organization of African Unity and one of Africa's most eminent diplomats, Salim brought skill and political weight to the negotiations. On the core political issues, he narrowed the gap between the two sides. There is still far to go. But, unless Garang's death reignites war in the South, peace is at least imaginable now.

Darfur today, though, is defined by ubiquitous abuse and human suffering. More than 2 million people are displaced. Another

200,000 are refugees. Hundreds of villages are destroyed. Although death rates have declined from the peaks of 2004, a huge population still lives from day to day and from hand to mouth, cut off from traditional livelihoods in wretched camps where survival is dependent on continued international interest and involvement. The famed resilience of Darfurians, supplemented by local and foreign relief aid, has averted an even greater disaster, but what has occurred is a crime as heinous as any described in international covenants.

The international response to the crimes that have been committed in Darfur – and that are still being committed, by forces that still enjoy impunity – has been too little, too late. There is, belatedly, a large, although precarious, relief operation. An African Union monitoring and protection force is being increased from 3,000 to 12,000 men. The UN Security Council has referred the case to the International Criminal Court, and has authorized targeted sanctions against individuals obstructing peace. But religious and racial extremism still disfigure the political landscape and the Janjawiid still roam free. A lasting settlement for Darfur will require more than today's emergency responses. Darfur needs massive social and economic development. It needs to find its proper place within the Sudanese nation. The enduring problems of the governance of the Bedouins, in Sudan, Chad and other Sahelian countries, must be addressed.

Despite the savagery of the past two years, many Darfurians still dream of putting their homeland back together, re-establishing ethnic harmony and reconstituting a social order that has been willfully destroyed. The task is huge, but the Sudanese people are wiser than their leaders. With their rights respected, and generous and sustained international involvement to oversee a return to the rule of law, the people of Darfur can still live a decent life together within their common home.

Julie Flint and Alex de Waal,
London and Cambridge MA, August 2005

I

The People of Darfur

Northern Darfur is a forbidding place. It has landscapes of elemental simplicity: vast sandy plains, jutting mountains and jagged ridges, and occasional ribbons of green along the all-too-rare seasonal watercourses. A village, sometimes comprising no more than a cluster of huts made from straw and branches, may be a day's ride from its neighbour. Every place, however humble, counts. A hand-dug well in a dry river bed can be the difference between life and death for a camel herd trekking from the valleys of central Darfur to the desert-edge pastures.

Darfur's people are resourceful and resilient. Extracting a living from this land requires unrelenting hard work and detailed knowledge of every crevice from which food or livelihood can be scratched. A woman living on the desert edge will know how to gather a dozen varieties of wild grasses and berries to supplement a meagre diet of cultivated millet and vegetables, along with goat or camel's milk. She will know the farms and village markets within a hundred miles or more, and will not hesitate to walk or ride such distances to buy, sell or work.

Nomads move 300 miles or more twice a year, ranging even further in exceptionally wet or unusually dry years. 'Settled' people

Market at Suni, Jebel Marra, in 1986, where traders and
nomads came to buy grain, fruit and vegetables

move also, migrating to open up new areas of farmland. In the
dry sandy areas of eastern Darfur, especially, villages grow and
die along with their water supplies and the fertility of their soils;
in the far south, along the forest edge, the frontier of cultivation
creeps southward every year. Mobility and distance make it difficult
to maintain authority: those in power must always contemplate
their subjects' option of simply moving beyond reach.

In the centre of Darfur, the extinct volcano of Jebel Marra rises
8,000 feet above the surrounding savanna. The green mountain
can be climbed in a day, an arduous trek through orchards, ter-
raced fields and pastures that reach nearly to the lip of the crater.
There are wonderful myths about the fertility of the soils on the
crater floor, and the monstrous creatures that live in the deep
waters of the crater lake. Jebel Marra is the greenest mountain of
Sahelian Africa, the only major watershed between the Ethiopian
escarpment and the headwaters of the Niger close to the Atlantic
Ocean. For many Darfurians this mountain possesses an almost
mythical quality.

Yet the historic centre of Darfur is not the highest peak, which lies at the southern end of the massif, but the drier, broken mountains further north. Five centuries ago, in the mountainous triangle between Kutum, Kebkabiya and Korma, centralized states were created. The first was the Tunjur empire, named for a people who still inhabit the region, and whose rulers' castles still stand abandoned on hilltops, ringed by long-dry terraces. The Tunjur remain an enigma: closely related in myth and language to the Fur, their history and ethnography has yet to be written. The successor to their empire was the Fur Sultanate, the first Muslim state in Darfur, which emerged in the middle of the seventeenth century. The region takes its name from the homeland (*dar*) of the Fur.

By 1800, the Fur sultanate was the most powerful state within the borders of modern-day Sudan. In adopting Islam as the official state religion, the Fur sultans also embraced Arabic as a language of religious faith, scholarship and jurisprudence. Both Arabic and Fur were spoken at court. Darfurians – like most Africans – were comfortable with multiple identities. Dar Fur was an African kingdom that embraced Arabs as valued equals.

Dor Village

The village of Dor lies north of Kutum, amid lumpy granite hills. It is drier and poorer than most parts of Darfur, but typical in the complicated allegiances of its people. In the middle of the eighteenth century, Dor was governed by a land grant from the ruler of Darfur, Sultan Mohamed Teyrab. Throughout this part of Darfur, even today, the chiefly families possess land titles in the form of documents, written on thick paper with a huge seal or stamp the size of a camel's hoof. This document is a *hakura*, or land grant. The term refers both to the grant and to the land itself.[1]

The *hakura* of Dor is known as Dar Sueini. The people are known as Kaitinga, and refer to themselves as *Koraberi*, which means

Fur women winnowing millet near Kutum, 1985

'Fur–Zaghawa' in both those languages. Most of the inhabitants
of Dor speak three languages: Fur, Zaghawa and Arabic, the latter
the lingua franca of Darfur.[2] The Fur are the largest group in
Darfur and Dor lies at their northern extremity; the Zaghawa are a
Saharan people, whose homeland lies on the Sudan–Chad border
at the edge of the desert. In the millennium-long dessication of
the Sahara, the Zaghawa have slowly moved southwards.

Like all Darfur villages, Dor is ethnically mixed. Twenty-five
years ago the village was dominated by four ethnic groups:
Zaghawa, Fur, Tunjur and Kaitinga. But some would argue that
Fur and Tunjur are parts of the same ancient group, and that
Kaitinga straddles all three. How could a person's identity be
pinned down? It depended on the context. For political allegiance,
blood-money payment and marriage considerations, ancestry was
most important. But that didn't stop almost half the marriages
in Dor crossing ethnic lines. In the marketplace, what mattered
most was which language was spoken. A smart merchant would
learn as many dialects as possible to gain the confidence of his
customers. When dealing with the district tax collector and magis-

trate, or using the wells to water your animals, what counted
was where you lived. If a Fur or Tunjur villager accumulated a
lot of animals and chose to move with them seasonally, he might
well prefer to call himself 'Zaghawa' or even 'Arab', in line with
his livelihood.[3]

A minority of Dor's residents were drawn from a host of
other ethnic groups: Seinga, Berti, Jawamaa and Masalit, plus two
categories of Arabs: Jallaba and Rizeigat. The Jellaba are traders
from the Nile. The Rizeigat are local Darfur Bedouins, members
of the Mahamid section, Awlad Tako clan. It's an impressive but
not untypical array of ethnic groups in one remote village.

Darfur is home to about 6 million people. There is just one
rainy season, lasting approximately from June to September, which
brings occasional storms to the arid north and regular showers
across the well-watered south. The best cultivation is in the central
belt, especially where big seasonal rivers, or *wadis*, run down from
Jebel Marra. But even in the semi-desert, there are hollows that
collect rainwater where millet can be grown. There is a span of
rural livelihoods, from the poorest farmers who have no livestock,
through farmers with sheep, goats and maybe a cow or two (the
majority), to purely nomadic herders. Camels do well in the dry
north, while cattle prefer the wetter south. There is a regular
cycle of boom and bust in the livestock economy, and as herders
acquire and lose animals and rely less or more on cultivation.
It was ever thus: the historical records are full of references to
settled Arab villages, and Arab sheikhs were granted land for
farming by the sultans as far back as records exist.

Dor lies close to one of just three all-season livestock routes
– known as *masars* – used by camel herders on their annual
north–south migrations. Six hours' walk to the east is Wadi
Sokhama, one of those rare seasonal watercourses that run north-
wards from Darfur's central plateau into the desert. Traditionally,
the nomads spent the rains and the following three months,
October to December, in the desert, grazing their camels on the

A Zaghawa herder
waters his camels,
near Karnoi, 1986

pastures along Wadi Howar, the last seasonal watercourse before
the desert, and further north, where the grasses known as jizu
are so succulent that camels can go without water for more
than thirty days. Until just a few years ago, this rich grazing
land was shared among Darfur's camelmen: Arabs, Zaghawa and
Meidob. In January, the herds move south, spending the winter
and dry season in the valleys south of Kutum or travelling into
the well-watered districts of south-west Darfur, along the three
major migration routes that everyone shares.

The people of Dor pay bridewealth and blood money in livestock, and – with no banks – animals are the store of wealth. At
this latitude, keeping a cow, a thirsty animal that needs lots of
grass, is little more than a vanity. Most of Dor's animals are sheep,

goats and camels, the latter traditionally entrusted to Arabs and Zaghawa herders for the northern migration – not forgetting the ubiquitous donkeys, essential for travel to market and carrying firewood and water.

A few days' travel north, along the seasonal watercourse that serves as the route to the autumn pastures, is a lake, known as Rahad Gineid or Gineik in Arabic and Zaghawa, respectively. In 1967 or 1968,[4] a fight began at Rahad Gineid between Zaghawa and Arab herders, the vast majority of them Rizeigat. It started over a livestock theft, and escalated into three days of armed encounters with rifles. The government intervened, and the subsequent court cases took two years to conclude. The chief of Dar Sueini, head of the Kaitinga, was selected as part of the mediation committee, on the Zaghawa side.

After this was over, the Zaghawa, Kaitinga and Tunjur ended their old practice of entrusting their camels to the Arabs, and Zaghawa herders took care of the camels from Dor. It showed a pattern which became more and more marked over the next generation: conflict divided groups along ethnic–ancestry lines. As the people of Dor say, 'conflict defines origins'.[5] Was this because people instinctively clung to their ancestral tribes in times of insecurity? Or was it because, when disputes came to be settled and compensation paid, corporate lineage groups were responsible for paying blood money? In short, was it the conflict itself or the means for settlement that defined 'origins'? The Gineid fight levered open a tribal divide. It was not inevitable: all Darfur's leading families have mixed ancestry, and 'origins' could have been defined in a different way.

Although the two sides at Gineid were Zaghawa and Rizeigat Arabs, the conflict was also related to an internal dispute within the Rizeigat – between the Mahamid and Mahariya sections. In our analysis of the origins of the Janjawiid, we will examine how this conflict played out over three generations, stoking the fires of violent conflict.

A History of Statehood and Ethnicity

A host of ethnic groups or tribes – between forty and ninety depending on one's definition – have emerged from Darfur's history. Dar Fur was an independent state for three centuries until 1916. It was one of the most powerful kingdoms in a string of such states positioned on the southern edge of the Sahara desert, trading with the Mediterranean and raiding their southern neighbours. When Napoleon occupied Egypt in 1799, he exchanged letters with the Sultan of Dar Fur, which at that time had a trade with Egypt five times the value of that with the kingdom of Sennar, Dar Fur's rival on the Nile. The Sultan was wealthy – the greatest merchant in the kingdom – and in principle possessed absolute power. At its zenith in the nineteenth century, Dar Fur's towns were prosperous: a visiting merchant, Mohamed al Tunisi, compared Kebkabiya favourably with country towns in Egypt.

The Dar Fur state was centred in the northern mountains, just south of Dor. The ruling clan here was the Keira dynasty, which gradually expanded its domain southwards. As the state spread its authority, it absorbed farming communities, which adopted the Fur language, adopted Islam, and came under the political and administrative suzerainty of the state. They 'became' Fur. During the eighteenth century, the system of *hakura* land grants was formalized and expanded. The *hakura* system is commonly described as 'tribal land ownership', but this is a misnomer in two respects. First, the system was not directly 'tribal', except on the southern peripheries of the empire. The *hakura*-holders were court appointees, entitled to collect dues from the people living in their domain. Often, the *hakura* head became a local potentate, building a base independent of the sultan, usually by collecting his kinsmen in the area. By these means the office became hereditary and the dominant group the tribe of the *hakura* chief. Hence the 'tribe' consolidated around the *hakura* as often as the other way around. Second, the rights of the *hakura* owner started off as feudal jurisdiction, and have never become freehold title. These subtleties are of more than historical importance: they influenced the political strategies of the land-hungry at the turn of the twenty-first century and help determine workable solutions for Darfur's crisis.

Only a minority of people within Dar Fur's dominions were, or became, Fur. There were also the Tunjur and Zaghawa in the north, the Berti and Birgid in the east, the Masalit in the west and many other smaller groups. The Masalit are especially significant. For centuries their villages were in the political no-man's land between Dar Fur and the Wadai Sultanate to the west, based in Abeche in today's Chad. Only in the late nineteenth century, as both these powerful states were plunged into crisis, was Dar Masalit able to emerge briefly as an independent polity.[6]

Darfur's Arabs arrived in substantial numbers between the fourteenth and eighteenth centuries. They fall into two groups: individual scholars and traders who arrived from the east and the west, and the Juhayna Bedouins who arrived from the north-west, in search of grass and water. The Juhayna Arabs trace their lineage back to Arabia and the Qoreish tribe of the Prophet Mohamed. Those who moved south of Jebel Marra took to herding cattle – becoming known as *Baggara*, or cattle-people – while those who stayed in the north remained as *Abbala*, or camel-men. In the sparsely settled south, the Fur sultans gave a large *hakura* to each of the four main Baggara groups, Ta'aisha, Beni Halba, Habbaniya and Rizeigat. Their Abbala cousins, moving as nomads in the densely administered northern provinces, occasionally received small estates, but had no jurisdiction over huge swathes of territory. To this day, many Abbala Arabs explain their involvement in the current conflict in terms of this 250-year-old search for land, granted to the Baggara but denied to them.

The Rizeigat are the largest and most powerful of the Arab tribes. Most live in south-east Darfur, under the political authority of the Madibu family. The Rizeigat in northern Darfur and Chad have the same ancestry but no enduring political connections. Their sections are Mahariya, Mahamid (which includes the powerful Um Jalul clan), Eteifat and Ereigat. Their camels made them rich and influential: they were Darfur's specialist export hauliers across the desert.

On its southern periphery, Dar Fur showed a different and more violent face. It was a slaving machine, hunting the forest peoples for slaves, both for its own domestic and agricultural economy and for export along the 'Forty Days' Road' to Egypt and beyond.

In the middle of the nineteenth century, attempting to carve out a slaving domain in Southern Sudan, the Fur raiding parties clashed with the mercenary army of Zubeir Rahma Pasha, the greatest of the Khartoum traders. Better financed and organized, Zubeir decided to invade the Sultanate itself. The Rizeigat of southern Darfur, recently centralized under Sheikh Musa Madibu, lay in his path. Correctly calculating that Zubeir would win, Madibu allowed him through. Zubeir succeeded in defeating Sultan Ibrahim Garad's army at Menawashei, south of al Fasher, but was then cheated out of his victory by the Khedive of Egypt, who summoned him to Cairo to discuss his triumph and kept him there. Darfur was annexed to the Ottoman Empire, Zubeir languished in Cairo, and his lieutenant Rabih Fadlalla cut loose with the mercenary remnants to begin a quarter-century of pillage across central Africa – a rampage that was ended only by his defeat by the French near Lake Chad in 1900.

Islam in Darfur

All Darfurians are Muslims, and the majority are followers either of the *Tijaniyya* Sufi sect, which originates in Morocco, or the *Ansar* followers of the Mahdi, or both. Islam was a state cult in imperial Dar Fur.

A particularly powerful Islamic influence came from West Africa:
Mahdism. In the 1880s, Sudan was convulsed by a messianic
revolution led by Mohamed Ahmed 'al Mahdi', the Expected
One. The Mahdi was a holy man from Dongola on the Nile,
who sought to bring about a new Caliphate. Frustrated by the
riverain sophisticates, the Mahdi turned to the west of Sudan. In
Kordofan, he met Abdullahi al Ta'aishi, an Arab Darfurian, whose
grandfather had migrated from the west. Abdullahi recognized
Mohamed Ahmed as the Mahdi, and in turn became his deputy
and successor. The two jointly defeated the Turko-Egyptian regime
and its mercenary generals (most famously, Charles Gordon),
and established a Mahdist state at Omdurman, across the river
from Khartoum. When the Mahdi died, the Khalifa Abdullahi
ruled Sudan for fifteen years as an efficient despot. His chief
lieutenants and much of his army, known as *Ansar*, hailed from
Darfur – especially from the Baggara, whom he moved en masse
to Omdurman and the White Nile to bolster his power.

The Khalifa Abdullahi was defeated by Kitchener's Maxim guns
on the plains of Kerari in 1898. One of his prisoners, a Fur of royal
blood, Ali Dinar, escaped to Dar Fur and restored the Sultanate,
describing his homeland as 'a heap of ruins'. The decimated
Arab tribes trickled back. While Sultanic authority was quickly
asserted in the central areas, the peripheries remained troublesome throughout Ali Dinar's eighteen-year reign. In 1913–14,
his attempts to consolidate his rule were set back by a serious
drought and famine, which gained the popular name Julu, meaning
'wandering', with reference to people's desperate migrations in
search of food. Ali Dinar's downfall was his miscalculation after
the outbreak of the Great War: anticipating an Ottoman victory,
he declared against the Allies. Concerned more by the example
of a rebellious province (Iraq was on the point of insurgency at
the time) than by any military threat, the governor-general in
Khartoum dispatched an expeditionary force which defeated the
Fur armies outside al Fasher and hunted down and killed the

fugitive Sultan shortly afterwards. In January 1917, Darfur was absorbed into the British Empire.

Thus ended four decades which, even by the sanguinary standards of Sudanese and Sahelian history, stand out, in Sultan Ali's own words, as an age of 'turmoil and bloodshed'. It was a period of exceptional dislocation and hunger, of unparalleled forced migration and wanton destruction. The only authority that survived was that which was able to wield unremitting force. The forced displacement of that era leaves many land claims disputed to this day, notably from Arab groups (including the Um Jalul) who were relocated to Omdurman or fled to Chad. Much is missing from the written and oral histories. The social historian Lidwien Kapteijns describes how one army marauding across western Darfur 'ate, drank, wore or stole' everything in its path.[7] One assumes that gender-based violence – rape – is absent from the record only because of the sensibilities of the (male) transmitters of oral archive.

Becoming Sudanese

Britain's only interest in Darfur was keeping the peace. It administered the province with absolute economy. The core of this was the 'Native Administration' system, by which chiefs administered their tribes on behalf of the government. Darfur's subtle ethnic politics and panoply of leaders needed considerable tidying up if a uniform hierarchy of chiefly authority were to be imposed. The British did their best, soon learning that they should leave alone what they could, embracing an array of titles (Sultan, Melik, Dimangawi, Magdum, Shartai and Fursha, to name but the upper ranks), and tolerating the idiosyncracies of local potentates provided that their abuses were not too egregious and they kept the peace. A new rank of Omda or sub-district administrative chief (and magistrate and tax collector) was introduced. The title Nazir was bestowed on Arab paramount chiefs – four in the south, two in the north,[8] but none for the Abbala Rizeigat, to their lasting chagrin. The Masalit Sultan, who had acceded to Sudan by treaty in 1922, retained his title and many of his judicial and administrative privileges. Along with the *nazir* of the (southern) Rizeigat, Ibrahim Musa Madibu, Sultan Bahr al Din Andoka of the Masalit was the most powerful tribal potentate in British Darfur. The Fur were politically decapitated, their landowning class reduced to penury, and – perhaps their greatest frustration – their contribution to Sudanese civilization reduced to a footnote in official histories that focused on the Egypt–Khartoum–South Sudan axis of politics and identity.

Only in 1945 did the colonial governor begin to consider possibilities for development in Darfur.[9] The file 'Economic Development, Darfur Province' in the Khartoum national archives, contains just five entries for the entire period 1917–50. Most bemoan the impossibility of doing anything except encouraging modest exports of cattle and gum. In 1935, Darfur had just one elementary school, one 'tribal' elementary school and two 'sub-grade' schools. This was worse than neglect: British policy was deliberately to restrict education to the sons of chiefs, so that their authority would not be challenged by better-schooled Sudanese administrators or merchants. In the health sector, things were no better. There was no maternity clinic before the 1940s, and at independence in 1956 Darfur had the lowest number of hospital beds of any Sudanese province (0.57 per thousand population – the next lowest was Bahr el Ghazal in the South).[10] The railway reached Nyala during the rule of General Ibrahim Abboud (1958–64) and the first metalled road outside a major town was begun in the late 1970s (heralded as the Nyala–Geneina highway, construction halted halfway, at Zalingei). When the first agro-economic studies were done in the 1960s, in preparation for two immense rural development schemes (the Western Savanna Development Corporation, based in Nyala, and the Jebel

Marra Rural Development Project, based in Zalingei), the first researchers and planners found themselves in virgin developmental territory.

Villagers in central and eastern Sudan complained that their land was taken over by commercial farmers armed with land titles and tractors. But they at least had a modicum of development. In Darfur, so distant from any sizeable markets, there was no investment at all. Most Darfurians who participated in the national economy did so as migrant labourers, following the old west–east pilgrimage route across Sudan to seek work in the irrigated farms along the Nile or the sorghum prairie farms of eastern Sudan.

Over the three generations from 1917, the people of Darfur 'became Sudanese'. They assimilated, almost entirely peacefully and voluntarily, to a Sudanese political, economic and cultural entity based on the River Nile. The most sympathetic insight into how this process operated at a local level is provided by Paul Doornbos, a Dutch anthropologist who lived in Foro Baranga on the Masalit–Chad border in the early 1980s.[11] Foro Baranga is a small town with a vast market that lies at the confluence of the three great watercourses that drain West Darfur: Wadi Azum, which originates in Jebel Marra; Wadi Kaja, which flows through Geneina; and Wadi Saleh, which drains the district of the same name. For eight months of each year, the three wadis flow into Chad, where they become the Salamat river, finally emptying their water into Lake Chad. Foro Baranga is green, fertile and wet, and is the southern terminus of the livestock migration route that begins at Rahad Gineid, more than 400 miles to the north.

Doornbos observed a process of cultural change that involved partial abandonment of Masalit culture, notably the independent status of women, tribal dancing, drinking *marissa* (millet beer), barter and traditional ways of dressing. All this was replaced by a new orthodoxy that included speaking Arabic, restricting the public role of women, using cash, dressing in the characteristic northern Sudanese manner, with *jellabiya* for men and *taub* for women, and shunning alcohol. Doornbos preferred to call this 'Sudanization' and not 'Arabization', for two reasons. First, the indigenous Arabs – both local Salamat and itinerant Rizeigat camel-men – were themselves changing their Bedouin culture to 'become Sudanese'. Second, the villagers did not aspire to become part of international Arab culture, but rather to be regarded as citizens of standing – and creditworthiness – by the dominant stratum of traders and officials. Doornbos identified several agents of 'Sudanization', including traders, administrators, schoolteachers and itinerant fundamentalist preachers. The pedantry of this sermonizing, and its hostility to the tolerant Sufiism of Darfur's older religious order, is captured in the edict of the preacher who denounced as 'hypocrites' 'those who use a plastic toothbrush and toothpaste rather than the seven kinds of twig claimed to be sanctioned by Islam'. Another thundered against drinking and sundry other evils, even as market-goers in tea shops turned up cassette-recorded music to drown him out. As so often, many conversions were short-lived. A well-known alcoholic stayed on the wagon for just three days, missing the companionship of his 'un-Sudanized' drinking companions too much. Poor farmers simply could not afford to cultivate without the hard labour of their wives in the fields. But the traders who had subsidized the preacher were content: those who had given up home-brewed *marissa* would now buy tea as well as expensive *jellabiyas* and *taubs*. The next day they raised the price of sugar to cover their outlay.

In Foro Baranga, thousands of Chadians mingled with Darfurians. They too were a mixture – Baggara Arabs from the Salamat tribe, Daju, Bornu and others. Many were becoming Sudanese in their own way, by the mere fact of settling down on vacant land on the edge of Fur and Masalit villages.

In the 1980s, the complaint of most Darfurians was not that the process of 'becoming Sudanese' denied them their own, unique cultural heritage, but that the government in Khartoum was not treating them as full citizens of the Sudanese state. Darfur's towns and villages had scarcely better services than in the days of the British. 'We are surviving here thanks to the grace of God and diesel engines', the sheikh of Legediba, a remote village in South Darfur, said in 1986.[12] Diesel lorries brought Legediba food supplies, and fuel for its water pump too. The sheikh knew that as economic crisis deepened and the price of fuel rose, traders would leave this small weekly market off their lorry routes. Sugar, tea and matches would run out and diesel for the pump would have to be rationed − pushing villagers one step closer to the edge. Darfur was a backwater, a prisoner of geography.

2

The Sudan Government

Emerging from the mosque on a Friday in May 2000, the faithful were met by young men quietly distributing copies of a thick document, photocopied and stapled. In tightly censored Khartoum, this was already surprising. But the contents of *The Black Book: Imbalance of Power and Wealth in Sudan* were more than surprising: they were revolutionary. They gave a detailed breakdown of where political and economic power in Sudan lay and documented how the state apparatus had been dominated, ever since independence, by a small group from the three tribes who live along the Nile north of Khartoum – the Shaygiyya, Ja'aliyiin and Danagla. The book showed that all other regions of Sudan had been grossly marginalized. Not just the South, which had been fighting for a better deal – or failing that, for separation – for decades, but also Sudan's eastern and western regions.

In three days 1,600 copies were distributed: 800 copies in Khartoum, 500 in other parts of Sudan (excepting the South) and 300 abroad. President Omar al Bashir and other top government officials reportedly found copies on their desks after their prayers. The contents of the book were further spread by government newspapers which denounced it on their front pages, reiterating government charges that the authors were 'tribalists'. Photocopies proliferated after the governor of Khartoum, Majzoub al Khalifa, ordered the security services to buy up every copy they could get their hands on.

The Black Book was the work of a group calling itself 'The Seekers of Truth and Justice'. Their meticulous statistics proved what everyone knew but never articulated: that the vast majority of government positions in Khartoum, from cabinet ministers to their drivers and all the bureaucracy in-between, were held by members of three tribes which represented only 5.4 per cent of Sudan's population. Demanding 'justice and equality', time and again, the Black Book showed that northerners were overwhelmingly dominant in the police and military hierarchy, the judiciary, provincial administrations, banks and developmental schemes. Every president had come from this region. Most senior ministers and generals too.

The Black Book roundly criticized the National Islamic Front government, which had seized power in a coup eleven years earlier. The NIF, the authors said, had 'demonstrated its inability to depart from established patterns of injustice, despite the slogans which it raised in its early days'. It had even portrayed jihad as a northern enterprise, despite the fact that the vast majority of martyrs were from Darfur and Kordofan. 'Examine with us the documentary films on Mujahidiin which are produced by the Popular Defence Forces and charity corporations', they wrote. 'Look at the pictures and scrutinize the names. Wouldn't you be certain that all the Mujahidiin in the Sudan are from the Northern Region?'

Sudan's Islamic Revolution

The Black Book was the obituary of the Islamic revolution of Hassan al Turabi and his acolyte-turned-archrival, Ali Osman Mohamed Taha. Just a few months previously, Ali Osman had sided with President Bashir in a power struggle in the leadership, enabling

Bashir to dismiss Turabi and impose a state of emergency. But criticizing Bashir's government did not imply supporting Turabi. The *Black Book* was compiled, in large part, by men who had joined the Islamic movement in their youth, convinced that political Islam offered a solution to Sudan's seemingly intractable political crises and failures of economic development. Just a decade earlier, the Muslim Brothers – the Islamists' core group – seemed to offer a new formula: they promised honesty, hard work and a commitment to the entire Muslim *umma*.

Tajuddin Bashir Nyam is one of many Darfurians who joined the Muslim Brothers as a student in the early 1980s. He supported their call for Islamic law but, equally importantly, he felt the Islamists overrode ethnic, tribal and societal divisions. He felt respected.[1] Darfurians were furious because Nimeiri had imposed on them, and only them, a governor not native to the region – a decision Nimeiri was forced to reverse after thousands of protestors took to the streets threatening 'a million martyrs or a new governor'. The decision convinced young men like Nyam that most northern politicians had a 'very bad image' of Darfur. But not Turabi. 'Even though most educated people in Darfur don't go to the mosque, Turabi had a close relationship with the people, a kind of respect for them.'

The Muslim Brothers won many Darfur youths over by the intensity of their involvement with them and their seeming lack of corruption. Darfurians were no longer being treated like hicks from the sticks, with contempt. Nyam:

> They sent people from Khartoum to speak to us, something other parties were not doing. Many of them were teachers. We found they were honest, very straightforward and with great morality. That was an important thing for us. They organized meetings once a week between people from the towns and the villages, people who had never met before. No one asked for tribes. They said: 'Islam is our mother and father.' They organized football teams and debates, and gave us books to read. We would read them, and then pass them on. This was

the opposite of what was happening at the time: everyone was taking everything for themselves. They gave us confidence and we were well respected by the community.

The Islamist activists focused their recruitment on youth, especially students. Their favourite targets were young men and women from rural areas who were bewildered and intimidated by the secular, impersonal culture they encountered on first arriving in the city. Sudan's traditional parties were content to rely on the rural aristocracy, while the Communists focused on the smart town kids. The Islamist leader, Turabi, had also studied the strategy of the Sudanese Mahdi, who, in the late nineteenth century, defeated the Egyptians and British to establish a theocratic state in Sudan. 'Hassan al Turabi had a prescient vision of Darfur', explained one of the most senior Islamists, Ghazi Salah al Din Attabani. 'He learned from history. The Mahdi had faced the elite of northern Sudan who rejected and ridiculed Mahdism. So he turned to the west and stormed the Nile from Kordofan and Darfur.'[2] Just as the Mahdi had forged his *Ansar* movement from the ranks of devout if unsophisticated western Sudanese Muslims, so Turabi saw that if his Islamist party was to win an election, it needed the votes of Darfur and Kordofan.

Turabi's 'western strategy' meant that he needed to break with the Muslim Brothers' exclusive orientation towards the Arab world. Along with their Egyptian parent movement, Sudan's founding Islamists had instinctively equated Islamism with Arabism. In western Sudan, however, they found Muslims who were not Arab. Ali al Haj Mohamed was one. Born in a village near Nyala, from the Bornu tribe which originates in West Africa, Ali al Haj became an influential Muslim Brother. His presence in the leadership held out the promise that the Islamic movement would be colour-blind.

For a while, the pledge seemed to hold. In the early 1970s, the Islamists fielded a Fur activist as their candidate for the presidency of the Khartoum University Students Union. Daud Yahya Bolad became the first KUSU leader who was not from the riverine elite. All previous KUSU presidents had subsequently followed an accelerated track to national political leadership. It seemed as though Ali al Haj and Bolad between them would win Darfur round to the Islamists.

Bolad's deputy and bodyguard was a medical student called Tayeb Ibrahim, nicknamed 'al Sikha' after the metal rods used for reinforcing concrete pillars with which he was wont to attack opponents during demonstrations. After leaving University, Tayeb 'Sikha' rose while his former boss did not. Bolad had no patron, no family ties to the rich and influential. The insidious racial discrimination of the Sudanese elite worked against him. Bolad returned to Darfur and tried to enter local politics. He flirted with the single party of then-President Jaafar Nimeiri, the Sudan Socialist Union, and was reportedly on Security's books. Bolad accused the Muslim Brothers of racism, a charge that the more thoughtful of his peers concede. 'The majority of the Islamists are from the Nile', Ghazi Salah al Din later reflected, explaining that treating non-Arab Islam as equal 'is not ingrained in their thinking. It is just a casual way of doing business.'

As Bolad lost his way, Ali al Haj remained a linchpin of the Islamist movement, and later the regime. When the Darfur protests forced Nimeiri to hold an election for the governorship, Ali al Haj stood for election. He was soundly defeated by the secularist Ahmad Diraige, a Fur. In the election, ideology mattered less than ethnic base: Diraige's was large, Ali al Haj's narrow. An internal memorandum commissioned by the Islamists after the election described the Fur as pious but introverted, and not a strong base for the Islamic movement. Thirteen years later, when Ali al Haj was Minister of Federal Affairs, he divided Darfur into three states, splitting the Fur constituency in hope of creating openings for Islamist candidates.

Daud Bolad, meanwhile, drifted further to the left. Former friends describe him as obsessive and driven, meticulously and energetically building up his political network. His frustrated ambition drew him to the Sudan People's Liberation Army, which, under the leadership of Dr John Garang, had been fighting for a 'New Sudan' since 1983. Although Garang's base was in the South, he was a strong advocate for national unity, arguing that the marginalized minorities of Sudan form a majority, and so should be entitled to rule. Garang attracted a loyal following among some northern Sudanese. The most notable of these was the Nuba leader Yousif Kuwa Mekki, under whose charismatic leadership thousands of Nuba from southern Kordofan flocked to the SPLA. Kuwa was more than a guerrilla; he was the leader of a cultural renaissance in which the Nuba asserted their 'African-ness' with new-found confidence. Bolad saw himself in the same mould. Garang, for his part, saw Bolad as the SPLA's opening to Darfur, another region with an oppressed and neglected 'African' majority. Other left-leaning Darfurian politicians, including Diraige, suspected that the SPLA would swallow them up, and stood aloof.

Letting Bolad slip away was not the only fateful decision the Khartoum Islamists made in this period. When they first formed a political party in 1964, the Sudanese Muslim Brothers resolved that theirs should be a wholly civilian movement. They had seen the debacle that overtook their Egyptian brethren in the 1940s after their leader, Hassan al Banna, created a 'Special Branch' within the movement which carried out a series of assassinations. Not only did this bring down the wrath of the Egyptian security forces – who shot al Banna dead – but the Special Branch then hijacked the Muslim Brotherhood itself, ousting the civilian leaders.

Yet in the bloody aftermath of the 1969 coup that brought Colonel Nimeiri to power, Sudan's Islamists turned to violence. The *Ansar* – followers of the Mahdi – led the way by establishing an armed stronghold at Abba Island on the Nile, and many Muslim Brothers joined them there. In March 1970, Nimeiri moved forcibly to crush the incipient uprising. Hundreds were killed in an air and ground assault, and the surviving leaders fled abroad and set up training camps in Libya. While Tayeb 'Sikha' was wielding his iron bar at university demonstrations, his comrades were undergoing military training in the Libyan desert. Their plan: an armed invasion of Sudan from bases in Libya, crossing Darfur and Kordofan to storm the capital. In July 1976, the Ansar–Islamist alliance very nearly succeeded, occupying much of Omdurman for several hours. Bona Malwal, the Minister for Information, rallied support for Nimeiri in a broadcast from Omdurman radio station. The army counterattacked and the rebels were defeated.

Libya's Colonel Muammar Gaddafi had his own plans for the region. He dreamed of annexing Chad as a prelude to establishing a vast Sahelian empire and spoke of an 'Arab Belt' or corridor into central Africa. He established an 'Islamic Legion' to serve as the vanguard of his military adventures, and recruited militiamen from Sahelian lands as far apart as Mauritania and Sudan. (His expansive definition of 'Arabs' included Tuaregs from Mali and Niger as well as Zaghawa and Bideyat from Darfur and Chad.) Gaddafi's rhetoric often far exceeded his capacity – his announcement of 'unity' between Libya and Chad in 1980 was not followed by practical actions to cement the merger. But his resounding statements and generosity with weaponry were enough to ignite new supremacist ambitions among the Bedouins of the Sahara.

Turabi, ever the opportunist, accepted Gaddafi's military assistance. He didn't trust Sudan's national army, with its tradition of secularism and hard drinking, and sought an Islamic counterweight. Numerous, devout and heir to a warrior tradition, the *Ansar* seemed the ideal footsoldiers for his Islamic revolution.

Turabi was impressively flexible. For him the means always justified the end – an Islamic state. In 1977, after the failed invasion, he made a volte-face: he made peace with Nimeiri. Back in Khartoum, he infiltrated Islamist cadres into the armed forces, including elite units such as the air force. (One of them was Mukhtar Mohamadein, an air force pilot who was the nominated leader for a coup should it be necessary. In March 1989, the Islamists' coup plans were thrown into momentary confusion when Mohamadein was shot down and killed over Nasir in Southern Sudan.) Tayeb 'Sikha', now a qualified physician, joined the medical corps. And, in what was possibly the most disastrous decision in the entire Sudanese civil war, the Islamists backed the 'militia strategy': the use of tribal militias as frontline counter-insurgency forces.

Counterinsurgency on the Cheap

The militia strategy began in July 1985, two months after the overthrow of Nimeiri. Alarmed at an SPLA incursion into Kordofan, and fearing that Garang would deliver on a threat to bring the war to the north, the transitional president General Abdel Rahman Suwar al Dahab, an Islamist sympathizer, resolved to step up the war against the SPLA. He dispatched his Minister of Defence, General Fadlalla Burma Nasir, to Kordofan and Darfur to mobilize the Arab tribes against the SPLA. In a series of meetings, General Fadlalla Burma selected former army officers and Ansar commanders to lead Baggara Arab militias, and provided them with arms and military support. In return the Baggara were promised a free hand to seize cattle and other possessions from the Dinka and Nuba populations suspected of supporting the rebels. Known in official parlance as 'Friendly Forces' and locally as *Murahaliin*, these militias became synonymous with atrocity. They sprang into the public eye in April 1987, when more than one thousand displaced Dinkas were shot and burned to death in the town of el Da'ien in south-eastern Darfur in retaliation for a series of battles in which the SPLA killed many Rizeigat militiamen.[3]

In Bahr el Ghazal in 1986–88, in the Nuba mountains in 1992–95, in Upper Nile in 1998–2003, and elsewhere on just a slightly smaller scale, militias supported by military intelligence and aerial bombardment attacked with unremitting brutality. Scorched earth, massacre, pillage and rape were the norm.[4]

Khartoum, meanwhile, did a deal with Tripoli: in return for weapons, the Sudan government turned a blind eye to Gaddafi using Darfur as a rear base for his wars in Chad. Thousands of Islamic Legion troops and Chadian Arabs crossed the desert to Darfur. Given the increasing local tensions, this sparked a conflagration in Darfur: an Arab–Fur war between 1987 and 1989 in which thousands were killed and hundreds of villages burned. An inter-tribal conference reached a peace deal in the same week that Omar al Bashir seized power. But Darfur's respite was short-lived. It soon became clear that Bashir, who strengthened the alliance with Libya, had no intention of enforcing the peace. Anger grew, compounded by official indifference to a major drought in 1990. The government's slogan 'We eat what we grow!' glossed over a disaster: economic policies that were causing hyperinflation and panic-buying of food stocks, and a foreign policy that had alienated the Arab world and the West, cutting off foreign aid.

Fur politicians such as Diraige had long predicted that Darfurians' patience would run out. Now Daud Bolad gambled that Darfur just needed the right leader to ignite a rebellion. In December 1991, a well-armed band of SPLA troops entered Darfur, with Bolad as its political commissar and Abdel Aziz Adam al Hilu, who hails from the Nuba Mountains but has a Masalit father, as its military commander. It was a fiasco. The force had to cross an expanse of territory inhabited by Baggara Arabs who controlled every water source. The SPLA presence was immediately noted and reported to the military governor, Doctor – and now Colonel – Tayeb Ibrahim 'Sikha'. Before Bolad and his force could reach Jebel Marra, a combined force of regular army and a militia drawn from the Beni Halba Arabs, known as fursan or 'horsemen', hunted them down and defeated them. The Beni Halba district town, Idd al Ghanam ('wells of the goats'), was renamed Idd al Fursan in honour of this victory. Dozens of Fur villages were burned in reprisal.

Bolad was captured alive, along with a notebook that contained scrupulous records of every member of his underground cells. He was interrogated by his former comrades and never seen again; his network was quietly and ruthlessly dismantled. The Darfurian resistance was set back by ten years.

In a note of contrition, the Black Book honours Daud Bolad as a 'martyr'. His political journey from the Muslim Brothers towards armed struggle for his people prefigured the same conversion by a later generation. In the late 1990s, disillusioned Darfurians began to abandon the Islamist movement in droves as the movement itself began to fragment. Beneath this power struggle was an ethnic–regional split: the Islamist securitate joined with the traditional riverine military elite to create a security cabal at the heart of the Sudanese state. There were no Darfurians in the inner circle.

Ali Osman Mohamed Taha, 'Hero of Sudan'

By 2000, Ali Osman had emerged as the pivotal figure in the regime. This is a man whose career encapsulates the entire history of Sudanese Islamism. He was born in 1948, the year Sudan's Islamists set up their first clandestine cells in Khartoum University. He is a Shaigiyya, one of the three controlling riverine tribes. He is from a poor family – his father was a zookeeper – but climbed to the top because of his talent, tribal connections and clarity of goals. He was leader of the NIF's parliamentary delegation during the democratic government of Sadiq al Mahdi from 1986 to 1989, but conspired to bring the government down when his agenda was blocked. For Musa Hilal, leader of the Janjawiid today, Ali Osman is 'the hero of Sudan'.[5]

In order for the coup against Sadiq to succeed, it was essential for the putchists to obtain the support, or at least the acquiescence, of Egypt and Saudi Arabia. If Turabi and Ali Osman were seen to be involved, that would be impossible. So Bashir portrayed himself as a nationalist army officer and created a Revolutionary Command Council, the sine qua non of a non-sectarian coup since Gamal Abdel Nasser. The NIF was dissolved, and Turabi and Ali Osman were sent to prison along with other members of the deposed government and parliament. Egypt and Saudi Arabia were fooled, but their fellow detainees were not. In Cooper Prison, the formerly feuding MPs reviewed their errors, and their feuds, and formed the opposition National Democratic Alliance. Ali Osman and Turabi were shunned. While the prisoners played football – parliamentarians versus trade unionists, with Sadiq al Mahdi, a fit 55-year-old, at centre forward – Turabi paced the touchline reading the Quran.

The pretence continued for months, even after the two Islamists were released into house arrest. The RCC met in daylight, considered its decrees and dispatched the relevant papers at nightfall to the private residences of Turabi and Ali Osman for scrutiny and strategizing. Turabi was the sheikh: aloof from the details, organizing the grand sweep of strategy. Ali Osman was the chief executive, scrutinizing the implementation of policy. The plan was for these two to remain in the shadows until the new regime was consolidated.

Because of Turabi's ambitious impatience, the plan didn't work out. In August 1990, Saddam Hussein invaded Kuwait. Turabi was no supporter of Saddam, but he saw this as the historic moment in which the Gulf monarchies would totter and Islamic revolution would sweep the Arab world. Brushing aside the more pragmatic policies of President Bashir, he declared for Saddam. In so doing, he not only revealed where real power lay, but opened the doors of Sudan to every militant in the Arab and Islamic worlds and condemned Sudan to a decade of isolation.

Turabi had revealed his pre-eminence in the regime, but still held no formal post in it. Ali Osman took the job of minister for social affairs. This was an interesting, and surprisingly powerful, position that revealed the regime's priorities. In the early 1990s, the Sudanese Islamists had embarked upon a project of social transformation even more ambitious than Nimeiri's leftist developmentalism. Under the rubric of the 'civilization project' (al Mashru' al Hadhari) and 'the comprehensive call to God' (al Da'awa al Shamla), Ali Osman set about a far-reaching project of creating a new Islamist constituency. Islamist cadres were dispatched to foment a new Islamist consciousness in every village. Islamist philanthropic agencies were mobilized to open schools and clinics, and to support the Popular Defence Forces. A raft of programmes aimed at building an Islamic Republic was launched.[6]

In 1995, Ali Osman was promoted to foreign minister, tasked with picking up the pieces of an ambitious foreign policy that had backfired. Turabi's gamble on an Iraqi victory in August 1990 was the mother of all miscalculations. After Desert Storm, Sudan had been shunned by Arab governments and embraced only by the militant fringe – most notoriously, by Osama bin Laden, who moved to Khartoum after being stripped of his Saudi citizenship. Sudanese foreign policy accordingly turned towards its African neighbours, in hope of exporting its Islamist revolution there. At first, everything seemed to go Khartoum's way. The first opening, which scarcely registered on the international radar, was the overthrow of Hissène Habré in Chad. The endgame of the Chadian civil war began with an attempted coup against Habré in February 1990. One of the three putchists, and the only one who escaped, was Idriss Deby, a military commander expert in desert warfare. Deby regrouped his forces in Darfur, but was routed, for a second time, by Habré's forces attacking across the border. Libya rearmed Deby, Khartoum assisted him by remobilizing 1,200 Chadian Arab militia, and France decided to look the other way. In December, Deby counterattacked and swiftly occupied N'Djamena.

Khartoum had several motives in backing Deby. One was to cut off a potential source of support for insurrection in Darfur. During the Fur–Arab war of 1987–89, Fur militants had made contact with the SPLA and opened an office in N'Djamena, where Habré was presenting himself as the African victor over Libya's Arab territorial aggrandizement. A second was the opportunity presented to remove armed Chadians from Sudan − both those in Darfur, who were running wild, and fighters of the radical Arab Conseil Démocratique Révolutionnaire interned in Khartoum. Third, Sudan now had a friendly and indebted government on its strategic western border: Deby, an ethnic Zaghawa, was close to leading NIF figures. Khartoum expected Deby to share power with the CDR and the Arabs fighters to remain there, rather than returning to Sudan. In the event, the CDR–Deby coalition was short lived, but the Chadian Arab–Khartoum alliance endured.

The other two regime changes that favoured Turabi's strategy were the fall of Siad Barre in Somalia in January 1991, which ushered in anarchy the Islamists could exploit, and the overthrow of Mengistu Haile Mariam in Ethiopia in May 1991. Guerrillas who had been extensively aided by Sudan in their long wars were now in power in Eritrea and Ethiopia − and they were favourably disposed towards Khartoum.

After this, Turabi and Ali Osman overreached. Their Popular Arab and Islamic Conference − a militant rival to the Arab League and Organization of the Islamic Conference − met several times, and the parallel Arab and Islamic Bureau sponsored a range of radical jihadist organizations across Africa. Having backed victorious rebel movements in 1990–91, they planned on repeating the exercise, only this time with ideological fellow-travellers. They aimed at regime changes from Cairo to Kampala, with the result that by 1994 they were engaged in mutual wars of destabilization with Egypt, Eritrea, Ethiopia and Uganda.[7] In June 1995, Sudanese-backed militants ambushed Egyptian President Hosni Mubarak's limousine as it drove down an Addis Ababa boulevard to the summit of the Organization of African Unity. The Egyptian leader had insisted that his special bullet-proof car be flown in for the fifteen-minute drive from airport to conference centre and he escaped unharmed. But the shock waves of the assassination attempt reverberated throughout the region. Sudan was sanctioned at the UN Security Council, its support for international terrorism exposed to all. A dozen foreign militants were named, including Osama bin Laden. All were expelled over the following twelve months.

The line of responsibility for the assassination reached right into the heart of Khartoum's security cabal. What goes on inside this close-knit group is impenetrable, but some on its fringes say that government colleagues remonstrated with Ali Osman, and accused him of running a state within a state. Egypt and Ethiopia drew up a list of those they considered responsible, among them Ali Osman and security chief Nafie Ali Nafie. This small, clandestine group had run training camps for international *jihadists*, hosted Osama bin Laden, and hatched a series of terrorist plots, using off-budget security agencies, accountable only to themselves. One of these agencies – known as *Amn al Ijabi*, or 'Constructive Security' – was using Islamic humanitarian agencies as cover for the militants' activities inside and outside the country. Their cover blown, several senior security officers were sidelined for some years. But Ali Osman, astonishingly, stayed in power and was foreign minister until 1998, when he was promoted – to the post of vice president.

Khartoum's foreign overreach was mirrored in the rise and fall of Turabi's and Ali Osman's plans for titanic social transformation. By the late 1990s, the Islamist project was imploding in military reversal, anger at the wastage of human life, and cynicism over the flagrant corruption of the leading cadres. But Turabi was undaunted. He succeeded in having his new constitution adopted in 1998 and became Speaker of the House. He formed a new single party, the National Congress. Apparently oblivious to the wreckage of his project, and ready to blame anyone except himself, he embarked upon a campaign of finally taking power for himself. By the end of 1999, it seemed that he had won every round and

that President Bashir was reduced to a figurehead. But Turabi
miscalculated in two areas. As he had feared in the 1960s, the
movement's security organs were loyal only to themselves. Also,
his lieutenant and chief implementing officer, Ali Osman, had had
enough of Turabi's recklessness. In December 1999, Bashir declared
a state of emergency and stripped Turabi of all his power.

The Bashir–Turabi split lost Darfur for the government, but
made it possible to make peace in the South. Bashir and Ali
Osman were no more accommodating than Turabi, but power
had finally been consolidated. And the two men who controlled
it knew they needed international respectability – not least to
attract investment and find a way of paying Sudan's $22 billion
debt. In 2001, a serious peace process began at last, seeking a
negotiated settlement to the civil war. The peace moves began
with a shift of US policy, in the first eight months of the Bush
presidency, in support of the peace process run by the north-east
African inter-state organization, the Inter-Governmental Authority
on Development (IGAD). The plan was to revive this almost
moribund process, under Kenyan leadership, with substantial
financial, technical and diplomatic support from Western powers.
No sooner had the framework been agreed than the attacks of
September 11 – by some of Khartoum's one-time protégés – made
Bashir prudently fall into line with US proposals.

For eighteen long months, government and SPLA delegates met,
argued and broke up. Ceasefire agreements were made, broken
and reaffirmed. The negotiations were lifted to a different plane
after Ali Osman came to the Kenyan lakeside resort of Naivasha in
September 2003 to talk directly with John Garang. But it still took
another fifteen months to hammer out a meticulously detailed set
of protocols. Negotiations continued right up to the last minute
before a final Comprehensive Peace Agreement was initialled on
New Year's Eve 2004. The signing ceremony in Nairobi on 9
January 2005 was disorganized, behind schedule and, because of
Darfur, anticlimactic. Yet it was a historic moment. A generation

of Southern Sudanese who had known nothing but war at last had peace within their grasp.

The Comprehensive Peace Agreement shares power between the existing Sudan government and the SPLM for a period of six years, followed by a referendum on self-determination for the South. John Garang is to be first vice president, Ali Osman to be second. Posts in central and state governments are allocated according to complex formulae. Blue Nile and South Kordofan, the site of substantial SPLA insurrections, are granted lesser regional autonomy. National elections are to be held before the end of the fourth year of the interim period. Revenues from the oilfields in the South are to be divided fifty–fifty between Khartoum and Southern Sudan. The current national army is to withdraw almost wholly from the South, handing over to the SPLA. 'Joint integrated units' consisting of the Sudan armed forces and SPLA are to be formed for the national capital.

The Naivasha agreement is a remarkably good deal for Southern Sudan. It is an attractive deal for retaining unity, yet has an opt-out clause. John Garang has every reason to be satisfied. But why did Ali Osman sign? The government was not defeated on the battlefield, and was gaining substantial revenue from oil – which it didn't have to share. Ali Osman tells his party that Naivasha is the best chance for unity, and preserves the gains of the Islamic revolution: Sharia law remains in the North, and the Congress Party keeps a narrow, 52 per cent majority of seats in the National Assembly. But the truth of the matter is that Ali Osman made concessions on peace in return for staying in power.

He did not count on the war in Darfur. Whatever legitimacy Khartoum's rule may have gained from the Naivasha peace deal has been vitiated by the horrors it was unleashing in Darfur.

3

The Janjawiid

The nomad encampment lay in the middle of a stony, trackless waste, three hours' drive from the district town of Kutum. Broad black tents were spread among the few thorn trees and in the distance was the great sweep of Wadi Kutum, its pale red sand ringed by date palms and vegetable gardens. Visitors waited on a fine Persian carpet while the sheikh was summoned. 'Actually he is *Nazir*', a paramount chief, one of his retinue explained, 'but Sheikh Hilal insists that he is called just Sheikh. Sheikhdom is from God, but its degrees are man-made.'[1]

Even in his eighties, bedridden and almost blind, Sheikh Hilal Abdalla was a commanding figure. As the visitors entered his tent, he swung his tall frame upright and ordered his retainer to slaughter a sheep for dinner. He was courteous and imperious in equal measure. 'Who are you?' he demanded. 'You can't be British. All the British speak Quranic Arabic!' It was Hilal who controlled the discussion that followed, reminiscing about Guy Moore and Wilfrid Thesiger, British colonial officers who spoke fluent Arabic, and praising Thesinger's skill in hunting lions – animals which had long since vanished from North Darfur. Then a servant served sweet tea on a silver platter while Hilal explained that the world was coming to an end.

Sheikh Hilal
Mohamed Abdalla in
his tent at Aamo, 1985

Although settled in Aamo for more than a decade, Hilal kept to the old nomadic ways. Hung on the sides of his tent were only those things that could be packed on the back of a camel in an afternoon – water jars, saddles, spears, swords, an old Remington rifle, his silver teaset and well-worn rugs. 'All the Um Jalul possess camels', he said. 'You see that small boy?' He gestured at his grandson. 'Even he has camels.' He spoke about the traditions of mutual support among the Um Jalul, the most traditional of Darfur's Rizeigat Arab nomads. During the famine which had devastated the region over the previous eighteen months, one of

his nephews had donated more than a hundred camels to support
hungry kinsmen. He himself had loaned many animals, from a
herd that was shrinking faster than he knew.

'None of us will need to cultivate', he said. 'None of us even
needs to collect wild foods like the Zaghawa. Camel nomadism
is our way of life.'

Yet just an hour's walk away was a small encampment of
destitute nomads whose animals were dead and who were scrap-
ing away at infertile, sandy soils in a desperate attempt to grow
enough millet to support their families. They pointed bitterly at
the distant wadi and its fertile alluvium. 'There's enough land
here', said one, 'but the Tunjur have registered every inch.' Their
cooking pots were filled not with millet but with wild foods,
especially the mukheit berries, bitter and scarcely palatable, that
had been the staple diet of most Darfurians during the famine
months.

The proud old sheikh refused to talk about his people's poverty.
Instead he spoke darkly of how the cosmic order was changing.
In the old days, the nomads had been welcome guests of the
Fur and Tunjur farmers. He himself had travelled south every
year to Kargula on the slopes of Jebel Marra, where the Fur
chief, Shartai Ibrahim Diraige, would welcome him with a feast
and the nomads would assist the farmers by buying their grain,
taking their goods to market and grazing their camels on the
stubble of the harvest. On leaving, the sheikh would present the
shartai with two young camels. But now all this was changing: Fur
farmers were barring the Arabs' migratory routes and forcing the
camel herders to range further south in search of pastures. The
masar – livestock migration route – that began at Rahad Gineid
now passed through Foro Baranga into southern Chad and the
Central African Republic.

In the far north, in Wadi Howar, the Um Jalul shared the
pastures with other herders, the Zaghawa and Meidob. But this,
too, was changing. The famous jizu desert pastures had bloomed

that season – 1985 – for the first time in seven years. Hilal brooded on the ecological changes that were disturbing the region. But he would rather die than change. For him, the old ways were the only ways. Contemptuous of police procedures, he presided over swift customary justice at his tribal court in Aamo. He had no hesitation in tying a witness or a suspect to a tree in the midday sun, or smearing him with grease to attract biting insects, to extract a confession. Punishment – payment of blood money, or whipping – was immediate. But people from many different tribes, in Chad as well as Darfur, trekked to Aamo court. There was no appeal, but the sheikh was famously just. The fame of his son Musa has spread even further: his name is first on a list of suspected genocidal criminals compiled by the US State Department.

Musa Hilal, A Big Sheikh

On 27 February 2004, hundreds of armed men mounted on camels and horses attacked the town of Tawila on the eastern slope of Jebel Marra, the heart of the Fur lands. By the time the attack was over, three days later, 75 people had been killed, 350 women and children abducted and more than 100 women raped,[2] including 41 teachers and girls from Tawila boarding school. Six of the women were raped in front of their fathers, who were then killed; some of the schoolgirls were gang-raped. Overseeing this mayhem, moving between a temporary headquarters in a large canvas tent and a convoy of five Land Cruisers protected by mounted men, was Musa Hilal, then 44, the most powerful leader of the government-supported militias that have come to be known as the Janjawiid. In the days before the attack, more than 500 Janjawiid had converged on Tawila from different directions and congregated, without interference from any of the government forces in the area, in a makeshift camp on a nearby hill. This was more than Arab raiders settling old scores.

Musa Hilal, 2004

These Janjawiid had light and medium weapons, communications, internal structure – and impunity. The state capital, al Fasher, is only forty miles away from Tawila and Governor Osman Yusuf Kibir was fully informed of the attack while it was continuing. But it was only on the third day, after the Janjawiid withdrew, that the governor sent representatives to Tawila. Video footage shows fly-covered corpses, charred and smoking ruins, and weeping women cradling terrified children.

Musa Hilal has denied being present in Tawila. But the attack was witnessed by hundreds of people and many recognized

him, even though he was wearing the uniform of a colonel in
the regular army. One, a retired teacher, hid in the bushes when
the attack began and took notes, feeling it was his duty as an
educated man to record what was happening.[3] He saw military
helicopters ferrying food and weapons in, every day, and taking
wounded out. 'Hilal moved and gave instructions, with men
unloading guns off of the helicopter... If you said you were
Arab he would say, "Come fight with me."'

Confident of the impunity afforded him by the government,
and of the international community's refusal to match its bark
with bite, Hilal has amused himself by playing word games
while his men burn Darfur. He has never convincingly denied
the crimes he stands accused of, nor shown any regret over the
destruction of Darfur, its people and its multi-ethnic society. He
has only protested at being called *Janjawiid* – a word customar-
ily used to refer to outlaws and highwaymen from Chad. 'The
Janjawiid are bandits, like the mutineers. It is we who are fighting
the Janjawiid.'[4] What Hilal does not deny, indeed relishes, is being
a government agent. 'A big sheikh... not a little sheikh.'[5] As the
father in his desert tent took pride in his independence, so does
the son in his Khartoum villa, many hundreds of miles away from
Darfur, take pride in being the government's man, 'appointed'
by the government to fight against the rebels. 'I answered my
government's appeal, and I called my people to arms. I didn't take
up arms personally. A tribal leader doesn't take up arms. I am a
sheikh. I am not a soldier. I am *soldiers!*' And not only 'soldiers'.
According to documents obtained by the authors, Hilal is also
leader – *amid* – of an Arab supremacist organization called the
Tajamu al Arabi, variously translated as the 'Arab Gathering', 'Arab
Alliance', 'Arab Congregation' and 'Arab Congress'. Little is known
about the secret organization of the Arab Gathering, which has
roots in Colonel Muammar Gaddafi's Libya and active contact
today, according to the documents, with 'intelligence and security
leaders' from other Arab countries. But its ultimate objective in

Darfur is spelled out in an August 2004 directive from Hilal's headquarters. 'Change the demography of Darfur and empty it of African tribes.' Confirming the control of Military Intelligence over the Darfur file, the directive is addressed to no fewer than three intelligence services – the Intelligence and Security Department, Military Intelligence and National Security, and the ultra-secret 'Constructive Security' or *Amn al Ijabi*.

In the figure of Musa Hilal, Arab supremacism has converged with criminal impunity, and the result has been cataclysm. Hilal's public position is that, at the request of the government, he raised a tribal militia to fight the rebellion in Darfur. This is true, as far as it goes. In December 2003, President Bashir vowed publicly to 'use the army, the police, the *Mujahadiin*, the *fursan* to get rid of the rebellion'. But there is more to Hilal's war than he acknowledges publicly. In the documents obtained by the authors, Hilal makes clear that he is doing more than merely combating a rebellion. He is waging *jihad*, 'cleaning our land of … agents, mercenaries, cowards and outlaws'. He urges steadfastness despite the spotlight focused on *Janjawiid* activities. 'We promise you that we are lions, we are the Swift and Fearsome Forces. We fear neither the media and the newspapers nor the foreign inter-lopers.' He sends greetings to his supporters, a roll-call of some of the most important men in national and regional government: 'Major General Omer al Bashir… *Ustaz* [learned man] Ali Osman Mohamed Taha, Vice President and the hero of Sudan… Brother Major General Adam Hamid Musa, Governor of South Darfur… Airforce General [Abdalla] Safi al Nur… Brother *Ustaz* Osman Mohamed Yousif Kibir, Governor of North Darfur' – and the man who turned a blind eye to the rape of Tawila.

Hilal signs himself 'The *Mujahid* and Sheikh Musa Hilal, *Amir* of the Swift and Fearsome Forces', the main division of the *Janjawiid* forces based at Misteriha, the *Janjawiid* control centre in North Darfur. He is not a common *Janjawiid* criminal. He is a holy warrior, tribal leader and commander-in-chief.

Without friends like Bashir and Ali Osman in Khartoum, Misteriha could not have expanded as it has since Musa Hilal moved there from Aamo in 1996. Twenty-five miles south-west of the garrison town of Kebkabiya, Misteriha lies close to a main road that is regularly patrolled by the army. In less than a decade, it has grown from a hamlet indistinguishable from its neighbours to a sprawling town with a helicopter pad, solid buildings, a huge mosque, a guest house and plans for electricity. Hilal's men get their marching orders from Khartoum. Khartoum may deny it, but Hilal doesn't. 'All the people in the field are led by top army commanders... These people get their orders from the Western command center and from Khartoum.'[6] The 20,000 men Hilal can reportedly muster, 5,000–6,000 of whom are based at Misteriha, are distinguishable from regular troops only by their sandals and turbans and the emblem, an armed man on camel-back, they wear on their jackets.

At the height of *Janjawiid* atrocities in 2004, a number of senior military officers and regional government officials were closely involved in the running of the Misteriha barracks. On the military side, they included General al Hadi Adam Hamid, head of the government's Border Guards, and Lt. Col. Abdel Wahid Saeed Ali Saeed from the army's Kebkabiya garrison. The director of Nomad Education in the North Darfur government, Abdel Rahman Abdalla Jadalla – son of the sheikh of the Eteifat section of the Rizeigat – was in charge of recruitment. The camp had about eighty vehicles, a huge number in this remote region. In early 2004, helicopters were landing in Misteriha daily, and sometimes even twice daily, offloading artillery, ammunitions, firearms, food and money. Recruits received a monthly payment of 150,000 Sudanese pounds, plus 20,000 Sudanese pounds a day for a horse or camel.[7] They could keep all the loot they could carry, with the exception of cash and heavy weapons, which had to be handed to Hilal.

Hilal's message to new recruits was that civilians from the same tribes as the rebels were also the enemy. '*Zurga* [blacks] always support the rebels.' One young Zaghawa volunteer ran away on being told that Arabs would attack civilian targets – villages – while non-Arabs like him would be sent to fight the rebels, their ethnic kin. 'We are the lords of this land', a *Janjawiid* leader told him. 'You blacks don't have any rights here... We are the original people of this area.'

How did Musa Hilal get from the tents of Aamo, where his father inspired such respect, to the paramilitary base that is Misteriha, where he commands such fear? The answer lies in a militarized ideology that fed off desperation and grievance.

Roots of the Northern Janjawiid

From the time of the Sultans, the camel-herding or Abbala Rizeigat had been a headache to the rulers of Darfur. They refused to stay in the places allotted to them, and had no paramount chief to keep them in order. The British authorities tried to tidy up the tribal hierarchies, but never succeeded. Since the Rizeigat camelmen were too few to qualify for their own *nazir*, the first plan was to put them under the authority of one of Britain's staunchest allies – Ibrahim Musa Madibu, *nazir* of the cattle-herding Baggara Rizeigat. But the Abbala were too far away from the *nazir*'s headquarters in south-eastern Darfur for that to be feasible. So the district officer proposed that the sheikhs of the Abbala Rizeigat elect their own deputy *nazir*.

The election, held at the annual horse fair in al Surfaya in December 1925, was anti-climactic. The most influential clans of the Mahamid, one of the main sections of the Abbala Rizeigat, boycotted the conference to protest against British support for Abdel Nebi Abdel Bagi Kiheil, a rival candidate. Abdel Nebi, elected in their absence, turned out to be ill suited for the post: he didn't have the wealth to provide the continual generosity expected of a leader, he quarreled with Ibrahim Madibu, and he preferred town life. A few years after the conference, he left his headquarters and court at Girer and Mahdi Hassaballa Ajina, sheikh of the Mahariya, became the most senior chief. But Mahdi never became *nazir*. His claim was disputed by the sheikh of the Mahamid, Issa Jalul, whose clan – the Um Jalul – was the richest and most numerous of the Abbala Rizeigat. No decision on the nazirate was possible without Jalul's consent.[8] Had Rizeigat camel-herders won their nazirate, a vast area of pastureland north of Kutum could have been allocated to them as a tribal homeland, ending their centuries-old search for land to call their own. Wells and reservoirs could have been dug to assist the herders in their annual trek northward to the desert, minimizing the risks of clashes with other nomads. But the status of the Abbala Rizeigat in Darfur's tribal hierarchy was never resolved, fuelling a cycle of tribal conflicts and economic grievances that culminated in the emergence of the *Janjawiid*.

In 1948, Issa Jalul died. None of his sons was considered worthy of succeeding him as sheikh of the Mahamid, and the clan leaders met to decide a successor. Hilal Mohamed Abdalla, then in his forties, came from a humble background: he had most recently been a guard in Jalul's court. But Jalul on his deathbed endorsed him as his successor and he was elected by acclaim. Hilal spent the following four decades striving to become the first *nazir* of the Abbala Rizeigat.

Sheikh Hilal and his Mahariya rival, Sheikh Adud Hassaballa, shared a court for fifteen years. But in 1963 the courts divided – Hilal moved to an encampment called Zeleita – and the two began competing for the allegiance of the smaller Rizeigat sections. Neither did well: the Ereigat and Eteifat established separate courts, and some subsections (such as the Awlad Bileil of the late Issa Jalul) went their own way entirely, relocating south to Wadi Saleh.

The Hilal–Adud rivalry took on party-political dimensions during Sudan's second parliamentary period, 1965–69, when the two men aligned with different parties. But what most effectively

The camel-herding Abbala Rizeigat of Darfur

Section	Subsection	Clan	Ruling family	Location of court
Mahamid	Awlad Sheikh/ Um Jalul	Awlad Mablul	Hilal Abdalla	Formerly Aamo, now Misteriha
		Awlad Bileili	Issa Jalul and Yunis Abdalla	Under nomadic *waha* 'oasis' administration
		Four other clans		
	Awlad Sheikh/ Um Seif al Din		Juma Mohamed	None
	Awlad Rashid		Adam Ja'ali	Formerly Muzbat, now Damrat al Sheikh
	3 other subsections			
Mahariya	9 subsections		Adud Hassaballa	Girer
Eteifat	5 subsections		Abdalla Jadalla	Um Sayala
Ereigat	5 subsections		Jibriil Abdalla	Misrih

stalled Hilal's ambition was fighting at Rahad Gineid in 1968, when Rizeigat camel herders clashed with Zaghawa pastoralists. A sheikh who could not control the violent proclivities of his followers stood no chance of becoming *nazir*.

The Abbala Rizeigat were disadvantaged even by Darfur standards. The only ones with fertile farmland were the Ereigat. Historically poor, not having camels, this small section had been given small land grants by the Fur Sultans. Although few in number and traditionally looked down on by their camel-owning cousins, the Ereigat now found themselves hosting their kin from other sections and gaining new influence. Few nomads were educated – families rich in camels did not send their sons to school – but

Um Jalul boys at Aamo, 1985

the Ereigat had an advantage here too. In the 1930s, District Commissioner Guy Moore had employed them in the police stables at Kutum, and several of their sons subsequently became policemen. One such was Ali Safi al Nur, whose son Abdalla became an air force general, friend of President Bashir and the most powerful member of the tribe in Khartoum. If the rural Abbala hoped that their cousins in the halls of government in Khartoum would bring them schools, clinics and deep boreholes for watering their camels, they were disappointed. Abdalla Safi al Nur and Hussein Abdalla Jibriil – son of the Ereigat sheikh who also rose to the rank of general, before becoming an MP – focused on building their own political careers.

Nimeiri's 1969 coup, and his abolition of nazirates two years later, put an end to Hilal's aspirations. Thereafter, Hilal's career focused on his court as a means of building a following. In 1973, he moved to Aamo, close to the Ereigat village at Misrih. It was a chance to build an alliance with the up-and-coming Ereigat, and to put Um Jalul boys into the Ereigat school. Hilal also sought to expand his numerical constituency by drawing into Darfur Mahamid sections from Chad, including the Awlad Eid from his own Um Jalul, clans from the Awlad Rashid and Um Seif al Din, plus the Awlad Janub and Awlad Zeid. To compete with him, Sheikh Adud encouraged immigration by Chadian Mahariya, whose largest subsection was the Awlad Ali. Twenty years later, in March 1995, each of these six groups was awarded an *amir* to reflect their new strength in Darfur and to swing the balance of tribal power in the favour of Arabs.

Recurring drought in Chad gave additional impetus to immigration into Darfur. In the 1970s a drought-stricken immigrant was asked by the head of Sudan's refugee commission when he expected to return home. He replied, 'Wherever there is land and rain will be my homeland!'[9] Again in the 1980s, not just Abbala Rizeigat but also whole clans of Beni Halba, Misiriya and Mahadi moved eastwards to join their kinsmen in a swathe of territory from the border of Geneina as far as Kebkabiya and Kutum.

Further south, the Baggara Salamat nomads were drifting eastwards too, seeking land and security. Small groups of cattle-herders moved up the Salamat River and crossed into Darfur at Foro Baranga. They set up camps on the edges of Fur, Ta'aisha and Beni Halba villages, joining brethren who had settled there earlier. They clashed with the Ta'aisha in 1982 over land claims, and lost. In Wadi Debarei, near Garsila and Deleig, the Salamat had no sheikh and selected a young man, Abdel Aziz Ali, as their spokesman, but he and his people were dismissed as Umshishi – 'savages' – by the local Fur. The Abbala Rizeigat who transited through the area didn't treat with them either. The numbers of Salamat grew slowly but inexorably, and by the 1990s they had thirteen *omda*-ships, but still neither nazirate nor *hakura*. Tensions were building.

Sheikh Hilal stayed at Aamo until his death in 1990. In his last years, he witnessed one momentous event beyond his control and

was caught up in another for which he was partly responsible.
The first event was the great drought and famine of 1984–85;
the second, the arming of his tribe.

The Death of the Old Order

Seeing the northern desert dying, and drawn increasingly to the
savanna to the south, the Zaghawa say that 'the world finishes
south'[10] The drying of the Sahara is an integral part of their
cosmos. The same is true for the camel-herding Rizeigat. They,
too, have drifted southwards across the desert over the centuries.
Speaking at the time of the great drought of 1984–85, Sheikh Hilal
recounted this historic migration, and how it had been driven
by drought, war and political rivalries: whenever two cousins
disagreed, one could always move somewhere else. Unlike other
Darfurian Arabs who claimed that their forefathers had always
come across an empty land, Hilal didn't dispute that Darfur
was always inhabited. Taking his stick, he drew a chessboard in
the sand. One set of squares he allocated to the Fur and Tunjur
farmers. The second set he labelled as pastureland, available for
the use of the nomads. But Hilal brooded on how the drought
was disrupting the age-old order: wind was blowing sand onto
cultivated farms and huge rainstorms were carving gullies out
of the wadis. Farmers were now barring the nomads' way by
erecting fences or even burning off the grass.

Even worse, although the old sheikh was too proud to admit
it, the Um Jalul were losing their beloved camels. Many were
becoming farmers or labourers in towns such as Kebkabiya and
Birka Saira, and the villages in between such as Misteriha. In 1985,
a food security assessment noted that the main problem faced by
the Rizeigat settled close to Kutum was the quality and quantity
of the land they had been allocated by the Tunjur, who held the
hakura, and the shrinking demand for daily labour on farms.

The road to Aamo

> The settled Rizeigat claim that they now have so few resources
> that they cannot outmigrate because they cannot afford the
> costs of transport and setting up new farms. ... There are some
> Rizeigat farms in goz [sandy soil] areas close to Birka Saira.
> Many of these have been abandoned due to declining yields, but
> there is currently an influx of impoverished Rizeigat ex-nomads
> into the area looking for work.[11]

The failed nomads of Aamo and Birka Saira, seeking a route
out of poverty, were ready conscripts to rapacious militias. Along
with the other peoples of Darfur, the Um Jalul were eating or
selling their precious assets in order to stay alive. Darfurians were
astonishingly resilient in the face of the worst threat to their
lives and livelihoods since the famine of 1913. Thanks to their
hardiness and skill, and especially to their ability to gather wild
foods, far fewer died than aid agencies predicted. But survival
came at a price which was only apparent later: they exhausted

their land, their assets and their hospitality. The fabric of rural life never recovered.

Sheikh Hilal was less innocent of the second change that killed the old order: guns. Just as the rains failed, semi-automatic firearms began to flood Darfur. Nimeiri had allowed Sudan's famine to develop unchecked and in April 1985 popular protests brought him down. Relief aid at last began to reach Darfur and, with a new regime in Khartoum ready to deal with Libya, the trans-Saharan road to the Kufra oasis in Libya was opened, transforming Darfur. The desert road allowed impoverished Darfurians to migrate to oil-rich Libya and send money back to their families. It also allowed *Ansar* and Islamist exiles to return to Sudan. Having trained in Gaddafi's camps, alongside the Islamic Legion or as part of the Arab Gathering, they arrived infused with a supremacist agenda. They also came with weapons: huge convoys of military trucks rolled across the desert to set up rear bases in Darfur.

Gaddafi's designs on Chad needed an intermediary in North Darfur. He chose the Mahamid, the largest section of the northern Rizeigat and the best represented in Chad. Sheikh Hilal, endeavouring to boost his clan's power, had long been in close touch with his brethren in Chad, and the Um Jalul's camps had been used for storing Libyan arms destined for the Burkan ('Volcano') Brigade headed by Ahmat Acyl Aghbash. But Hilal never saw the new automatic weapons that changed the face of Darfur. Incapacitated from early 1986, the old sheikh lost his sight, rarely rose from his bed, and withdrew from worldly affairs. Three candidates competed for the leadership of the Mahamid – two of his sons and Ishaq Issa Jalul, son of the man that Hilal had himself challenged forty years earlier. Musa, the only one of Sheikh Hilal's sons who had attended secondary school, was chosen. As clashes with the Fur grew more frequent, it was he who organized the Mahamid's new arms supplies from Libya.

The Kalashnikov rifle transformed the moral order of Darfur. The Bedouins had lived by a moral code that included loyalty, hospitality, strenuous self-discipline when herding camels, and communal responsibility for homicide. The principle of paying *diya*, or blood money, to the kin of an individual killed in a feud ensured that violence was a collective responsibility. In the era of spears and swords, and even the early rifles, a killing was a deliberate and individual act readily traceable to the man responsible. Fights rarely had more than a handful of fatalities. The AK-47 – capable of slaughtering an entire platoon, truckload of passengers, or family – swept this aside. Blood money for a single massacre could be the camel wealth of a whole lineage. The sheer number of bullets fired made it impossible to ascertain who had shot whom. Young men with guns were not only able to terrify the population at large, but were free of the control of their elders.

By the time Sheikh Hilal Abdalla died in 1990, a Kalashnikov could be bought for $40 in a Darfur market. A jingle of the time ran: 'The Kalash brings cash; without a Kalash you're trash.' Armed robbery was rife. The regional government in al Fasher had neither the resources nor the will to control the crime epidemic: its camel-mounted police with their colonial-era rifles were massively outgunned by the new bandits. It tried to compensate for the rarity with which it caught criminals by the savagery of the punishments it meted out, including amputation and crucifixion – the public display, on gallows at town entrances, of hanged corpses.

The Arab Gathering

As significant as lack of rain and an abundance of guns was a new political ideology in Darfur: Arab supremacism. Sheikh Hilal, for all his stature and ambition, was a parochial and traditional man; neither he nor his courtiers had ideological sophistication. But by the end of the 1980s, the old Bedouin intrigues became caught up in national and international currents far stronger than they. The origins of those currents lay in the Libya of Colonel Gaddafi in the 1970s. The roots of Arab supremacism in Darfur do not lie in the Arabized elite ruling in Khartoum. They lie in the politics of the Sahara.

In Sudan in the 1960s, the Umma Party and the Muslim Brothers had supported with arms, money and rear bases the Arab factions that led the Chadian opposition, believing that they were fighting for the rights of Muslims against the Chadian government's Christian, 'African' agenda. But Nimeiri normalized relations with Chad on coming to power in 1969 and the axis of Sahelian Arabism shifted to Libya, where Colonel Gaddafi was dreaming of an Arab state straddling the desert and where, thanks to oil money, he was busy fashioning his instruments. These included the *Failiq al Islamiyya* (Islamic Legion), which recruited Bedouins from Mauritania to Sudan; the *Munazamat Da'awa al Islamiyya* (Organization of the Islamic Call), which fostered Islamic philanthropy and evangelization; and sponsorship of the Sudanese opposition National Front including the Muslim Brothers and the *Ansar*, the *umma*'s military wing. In addition, Gaddafi was hosting a raft of Arab opposition movements, known popularly as the 'Arab Gathering', and giving them military training in Kufra in the south-east of the country.

Gaddafi's own immediate interest was Chad, a first step in his plan to establish an Arab 'belt' across Africa. In 1975, he formally annexed the Aozou Strip in northern Chad. In 1976, he sponsored a National Front invasion of Sudan across the desert, which failed. By 1979, Libyan troops were fighting in N'Djamena. In 1981, Gaddafi proclaimed the unity of Libya and Chad.

Libya was vigorously opposed by the United States and France, who backed not only the Chadian leader Hissène Habré but also President Nimeiri in Khartoum. When Habré was briefly out of power in 1981–83, he retreated to Darfur, whence, rearmed with Sudanese support, he marched to N'Djamena and reclaimed power. Gaddafi redoubled his efforts to get rid of Habré, and when his rival and antagonist Nimeiri was overthrown in 1985, quickly cut a deal with the successor government. In return for oil and weapons for Khartoum's war in the south, Libya was allowed to use Darfur as the back door to Chad. Gaddafi's leading Chadian protégé was Acheikh Ibn Omar Saeed, who had taken over the opposition Conseil Démocratique Révolutionnaire (CDR) and its armed wing, the Burkan Brigade, in 1982 after Ahmat Acyl stepped backwards into the propeller blades of his Cessna aeroplane. Acyl had forged a military alliance between his own Salamat militia and the Mahamid Abbala. Ibn Omar, more than a warlord, was an Arab supremacist.

In Darfur, the first signs of an Arab racist ideology emerged in the early 1980s. At the time of regional elections in 1981, candidatures had taken on ethnic dimensions and the Arabs had been hopelessly split, allowing the Fur politician Ahmed Diraige to sweep to power. Darfurian Arabs argued that if they were united, and drew the Zaghawa and Fellata into their constituency, they could command an absolute majority. All that was needed was an 'Arab Alliance'. Around this time, leaflets and cassette recordings purporting to come from a group calling itself the Arab Gathering began to be distributed anonymously, proclaiming that the *zurga* had ruled Darfur long enough and it was time for Arabs to have their turn. The speakers claimed that Arabs constituted a majority in Darfur and should therefore prepare themselves to take over the regional government – by force if necessary. The name Darfur, the 'homeland of the Fur', should be changed to reflect the new reality.

The notion of Arab superiority had been a feature of northern Sudanese society for centuries, but this was something new. This was militant and inflammatory. With Darfur generally calm, and inter-tribal relations generally good, most officials dismissed the 'Arab Gathering', whatever it was, as a lunatic fringe. But in February 1982 an attack took place that forced a reassessment. Armed men cordoned off the weekly market in Awal, near

Kebkabiya, and ordered everyone to lie on the ground. They demanded to know which tribes their victims belonged to. Arabs were allowed to take their belongings and leave; non-Arabs were robbed, beaten and kicked. Security reports on the incident said the bandits wore army uniforms and carried modern firearms.[12] Similar events, although on a smaller scale, occurred in other villages around Jebel Marra. The victims were always Fur or other non-Arabs, never Arabs.

On 5 October 1987, the Arab Gathering emerged from the shadows for the first time with an open letter to Prime Minister Sadiq al Mahdi written by twenty-three prominent Darfur Arabs – three of whom later claimed that their names had been used without their consent. Published in the independent al Ayam newspaper, and signed in the name of the 'Committee of the Arab Gathering', the letter was an unsettling mixture of familiar political demands and supremacist claims. It claimed that Arab tribes represented more than 70 per cent of Darfur's total population and were politically, economically and socially 'predominant'. Despite this, they had been 'deprived of true representation in the leadership of Darfur region'. The signatories called for decentralization and regional administrative reform, and 'requested' 50 per cent of all government posts in the region. They called upon al Mahdi to assist them, as 'one of their own.' This much was the standard fare of competitive politics. But the letter ended in more sinister fashion:

> Should the neglect of the Arab race continue, and the Arabs
> be denied their share in government, we are afraid that things
> may escape the control of wise men and revert to ignorant
> people and the mob. Then there could be catastrophe, with dire
> consequences.

A few months later, in response to Sadiq's choice of Tijani Sese, a Fur, as governor of Darfur, an unsigned directive from the Executive Committee of the Arab Gathering, a committee not heard of before, enjoined Darfur's Arabs to 'cripple' Sese's regional government. Marked 'Top Secret', the directive said 'volunteers' should be infiltrated into *zurga* areas 'to stop production in these areas, to eliminate their leaders' and to create conflicts between *zurga* tribes 'to ensure their disunity'. 'All possible means' should be used to disrupt *zurga* schools. Along with a manifesto of the same date, which came to be known as Qoreish 1, this was a battle plan for the *Janjawiid*.

A second directive, published during the 'critical stage' of 1998–99, laid out the aims and strategies of the movement in greater detail, and set a 'target date' of 2020 for completion of its project. Invoking the name of the tribe of the Prophet Mohamed, this directive was entitled 'Qoreish 2'. The crux of Qoreishi ideology, a convergence of Arab supremacy and Islamic extremism, is that that those who trace their lineage to the Prophet Mohamed are the true custodians of Islam and therefore entitled to rule Muslim lands. Adherents regard Sudan's riverine elite as 'half-caste' Nubian–Egyptians and believe the country's only authentic Arabs are the Juhayna, the direct descendents of the Qoreish, who crossed the Sahara from Libya in the Middle Ages. They claim that these immigrants found an empty land stretching from the Nile to Lake Chad, and say this land should now be governed by their descendants – the present-day Abbala and Baggara Arabs.

Although a jumble of ambitions and racist claims devoid of intellectual sophistication, 'Qoreish 2' nonetheless laid out an agenda for taking power. At national level, it proposed feigning 'collaboration' while secretly infiltrating the Congress Party, government and all the institutions – political, economic, security and military – of the 'hybrid' riverine tribes that 'have been an obstacle for us for more than a century'. It also set out a plan for dominating Darfur and Kordofan by cooperating tactically with non-Arab tribes including the Dinka of Southern Sudan. It proposed securing 'sufficient pastures for nomads in Sudan, Chad, and the Central African Republic' and stressed the importance of 'strategic understanding with Libya' and the 'brothers in Gulf States'.

The Arab Gathering had sympathizers in Khartoum from the start. But the true ideological bedfellow – specifically mentioned in 'Qoreish 2' – was Acheikh Ibn Omar. Ibn Omar's CDR – a wild gang of Bedouins – was already better armed and more mobile than any Sudanese force.

Ibn Omar's first base in Darfur was a refugee camp at Anjikoti, adjacent to the teeming border market of Foro Baranga. More than three-quarters of the 27,000 refugees, who began arriving in 1983, had started farming locally, joining more than 10,000 kinsmen already settled in the area. Almost all illiterate, the Chadians had few opportunities in Sudan, but even worse prospects back home, where they felt that Habré's Goraan tribe nursed a visceral hatred of Arabs. For these refugees, neglect by Khartoum was infinitely preferable to N'Djamena's regime of institutionalized robbery and arbitrary violence. Parts of Wadi Saleh district were becoming Chadian enclaves. A survey by UNHCR found that only 3 per cent were prepared to go back to Chad.[13] But these simple rural people, seeking security and a modest livelihood, were denied the chance to live in peace. Anjikoti was also a magnet for Chadian dissidents, who recognized its strategic location – close to the biggest mercantile centre in the border zone, on the Abbala migration route, and the water source for eastern Chad – and set up an armed camp. The first violent displacement of Fur villagers occurred here. Twenty years later, they are still displaced around Nyala, known as *Jimjaabu* – 'the rifle brought them'. After Anjikoti was attacked by Chadian troops and French special forces, Ibn Omar moved deeper into Darfur and set up camp with the Islamic Legion in the mountains near Kutum, where Habré's Toyota-mounted fighters and French jets chased him again.

The Qoreishi idea became an ideology in arms. No sooner had it been published than Darfur was engulfed in a civil war that was stoked by the spillover from Chad. Fighting began in mid-1987, intensified with an assault on Jebel Marra in March 1988, and continued until May 1989.[14] The Beni Halba of Nazir al Hadi Issa Dabaker were actively engaged and also the Um Jalul of Musa Hilal, who contemporaries say was telling the Arabs of North Darfur: 'Fight – or lose your land and be destroyed.' For the first time, Darfurians heard of a militia called Janjawiid – a word that means 'hordes' or 'ruffians', but also has echoes of the Arabic words jim (the letter 'G', referring to the G3 rifle), jinn (devil) and jawad (horse).

The Fur militia made contacts with Habré's government and began smuggling in their own weapons. For eighteen months, the Khartoum government simply denied the problem. Darfurians organized large peaceful protests in Khartoum and three Fur MPs elected on the NIF ticket resigned their party whip in protest, claiming there was 'a conspiracy to reshape Darfur and open it up for foreign resettlement' by those seeking to overthrow the N'Djamena government.[15] Many Darfurian Arabs also recognized the disastrous path that regional politics were taking. But Khartoum was still reluctant to acknowledge the war, and only supported a peace conference, in al Fasher, when Gaddafi momentarily lost interest in Darfur.

In March 1987, Chadian forces smashed the Libyan army in the battle of Ouadi Doum in the Chadian Sahara, forcing Gaddafi to make an abrupt reversal of policy and recognize the Habré government. Ibn Omar was caught by surprise and quickly sought peace with his arch-enemy too. As a history of the thirty-year Sahara conflict says: 'Ideology, principle and even honor were no substitute for self-preservation by the chieftains of the Sahara.'[16] The defeated CDR distributed its arms to its local Darfurian allies. Tijani Sese, governor of Darfur at the time, already regarded Sheikh Musa Hilal as a troublemaker, a hothead who 'was inciting tribal hatred and conflict'.[17] Army Intelligence in al Fasher began investigating him, concerned by his destabilizing activities, and

in 1988 taped a meeting between him and representatives of
Ibn Omar in al Fasher. Musa Hilal, the governor says, was heard
thanking Ibn Omar's men for 'providing his tribe in Sudan with
the necessary weapons and ammunition to exterminate the African
tribes in Darfur'. Sese sacked Hilal from his position as sheikh.

In May 1989, Governor Sese succeeded in convening a peace
conference in al Fasher, with the Masalit Sultan, Abdel Rahman
Bahr al Din Andoka, as principal mediator. At the conference,
the Fur claimed 2,500 of their people had been killed, 400
villages burned and 40,000 head of livestock stolen. The Arab
side claimed 500 deaths, 700 tents and houses destroyed and
3,000 livestock lost. Each side accused the other of being driven
by ethnic exclusivism, of trying to establish, respectively, an
'Arab belt' and an 'African belt' in Darfur. The speeches and a
reconciliation agreement signed on 8 July 1989, days after the 30
June coup that brought Brigadier Omer al Bashir to power, all
stressed the local dimensions of the conflict.[18] The tribal leaders
glossed over the political–ideological dimensions of the war.
The agreement called for restitution and compensation, mutual
disarmament, the deportation of illegal aliens – Chadians – and
a host of measures concerning pasture, water, local land rights
and return of displaced people. It identified the collapse of local
government and policing as a major problem and called for the
disarming of Fur self-defence groups and Arab Janjawiid – the first
official use of the name.

However, hopes of peace were short-lived. The peace deal was
not implemented, and Darfurian politics continued to polarize.
Gaddafi and the Sudanese Islamists had common agendas – not
least a $250 million weapons deal. Shortly after the NIF's take-
over, the two leaders announced ambitious plans for cooperation,
including free movement of people between their countries. The
convergence was ideological too. In a statement with distinct
echoes of Qoreishi beliefs, Gaddafi emphasized the unity of
Arabism and Islamism, saying 'We [the Arabs] are the Imams. We

are responsible for Islam, which was revealed in our language. It is our book and our prophet alone. We do not accept a foreigner to come to us with his ideas.'[19]

The Masalit War:
'The beginning of the organization of the Janjawiid'

Drought and destitution embittered the Darfur Arabs. Weapons and a self-asserting ideology gave them new aggression and confidence. They were ripe for picking by the government, which began to harness them as a proxy instrument of military control. In the beginning, Khartoum's use of tribal militias was purely opportunistic: they were there, they had fighting skills and they allowed the government to conserve its own, overstretched resources. But as time went on, and *jihad* was unleashed, the militias served a second, equally important function: they gave the government the cover of 'age-old tribal conflict', enabling it to deny there was a civil war at all.

The militia strategy was well entrenched by the time Daud Bolad led SPLA forces into South Darfur in 1991. With few regular troops in the region, it was predictable that the government would turn to Arab militias for help. The Beni Halba *fursan* obliged and played the leading role in routing Bolad's force. Army and *fursan* burned entire villages on suspicion of having welcomed Bolad's men. The military governor of Darfur, Colonel Tayeb Ibrahim, was anxious to ensure that the reprisals did not spark a wider war. He had learned the lesson of South Kordofan, where government overreaction had driven the Nuba into the arms of the SPLA. For two years, he tried to keep Darfurians within the Islamist movement, publicly complimenting the Fur for their piety and assuring them that loyalty would have its rewards.

The governor's hearts-and-minds campaign temporarily put out the fires. But in 1994, the minister for federal affairs, Ali al

Haj, redrew the administrative boundaries of Darfur as part of
a constitutional reform that created a pseudo-federal system of
administration across Sudan. From being a single region, Darfur
was divided into three administrative states – North Darfur, with
its capital in al Fasher; West Darfur, centred on Geneina; and South
Darfur, on Nyala. The reform divided the Fur, the largest tribe in
Darfur, among the three new states, making them minorities in
each and significantly reducing their influence. It formalized the
tribal hierarchy, including a system whereby each tribal administrator was chosen by a majority of those from the rank below. Most
problematically, it created a raft of new positions – and gave almost
all to Arabs, rewarding allies such as the Beni Halba and Chadian
Arabs. Previously, Dar Masalit district had a sultan – a hereditary
post in the Andoka family – and five furshas, administrative chiefs
with land jurisdiction. Now, eight new amirs were appointed. All
were Arabs, although they represented at most one-quarter of the
population, and most were relative newcomers from Chad. The
then governor of West Darfur, Ibrahim Yahya, recalls that 'Omar
Bashir came to Geneina and personally gave flags to Arab amirs.'[20]
A law organizing the 'Native Administration' stipulated that the
sultan would be 'elected by the electoral college that consists of
all the furshas and amirs subject to the Sultanate'.[21] His term was
limited to seven years, or as long as the state government should
determine. The implication was clear: the Masalit sultan would
in due course be replaced by an Arab candidate.

The Masalit chiefs lost much of their legislative, judicial and
tax-collecting powers, crippling the traditional system of dispute
settlement. The Arab amirs were not formally given hakuras, but
their senior titles clearly implied they had the right to claim land.
Qoreish 2, Section A15, specifies: 'Take a strong negative stand
against land tenure systems (hakuras, dars) by all methods.'

This agenda of Arab domination was assertively promoted by
Mohamed al Amin Salih Baraka, a 'nomad MP' in the national
parliament. Voluble and restless, Mohamed al Amin Baraka looks

more like a political pundit than a politician. And indeed he was editor-in-chief of *Al-Bouhaira* newspaper in N'Djamena in 1990, when the CDR was briefly part of Chad's ruling coalition. After coming to Sudan in 1994 – where his brother Bashir was appointed as *amir* of the Awlad Ali subsection of the Mahariya – Mohamed al Amin Baraka became treasurer of the Herders' Union and then MP. None of this could have happened without the direct backing of powerful friends in Khartoum. Evasive about his background, he is aggressive in his disregard for Darfurian sensibilities over such basic pillars of society as the *hakura* system. 'The *government* owns all the land', he insists. 'Much of it is empty and not used, and things have changed since the *hakura* system was set up. The *hakura* is not a Bible, and it should be replaced by a new law to organize the land.'[22]

As unrest grew in West Darfur, the government began arming proxies. A military man, Maj. Gen. Hassan Suleiman, replaced the civilian governor, Mohamed al Fadul, and began arming the Arab *amirs*, among them Hamid Dawai, a Mahamid, and Abdalla Abu Shineibat of the Abbala Beni Halba. Prominent members of the Masalit community were arrested, imprisoned and tortured; Masalit civilians were disarmed, placed under curfew and restricted in their movements; Masalit youths were forcibly conscripted and sent to Southern Sudan to fight. In a three-year war, 1996–98, hundreds of civilians were killed, most of them by government-backed militias. Another 100,000 fled to Chad. A contemporary report described the militias' modus operandi:

> Most attacks took place late at night, when villagers were sleeping. Upon reaching a village, the attackers typically began by setting fire to all the houses. Villagers who managed to escape the flames were then shot by the Arab militias as they fled their homes. The timing of most attacks coincided with the agricultural harvest. By burning the fields just before they were ready to be harvested, or while the crop lay on the ground after first being cut, the militias destroyed the year's crop and exposed

Masalit farmers to starvation.... The atrocities were well planned, and directed by the Sudanese military governor of the area.[23]

This was, according to Ibrahim Yahya, 'the beginning of the organization of the Janjawiid' by the government. 'The army would search and disarm villages, and two days later the Janjawiid would go in. They would attack and loot from 6 a.m. to 2 p.m., only ten minutes away from the army. By this process all of Dar Masalit was burned.'[24] Yahya challenged an army leader, and was told: 'They are only doing their duty.' So he went to Khartoum, where he met Bashir and Ali Osman. He asked them why the army was taking its orders directly from Khartoum. Their answer was: 'You Africans are not reliable.'

As Masalit resistance solidified, the government reinforced the Arab militias. In 1999, Mohamed Ahmad al Dabi, a Shaygiyya general in military intelligence, was despatched to Geneina as personal representative of President Bashir – officially, to restore calm. An established militia under Dabi's control, the Quwait al Salaam or Peace Forces, was moved to South Darfur. Drawn from South Kordofan Arabs, the Peace Forces had been deployed to protect trains and convoys crossing into Southern Sudan. Quartered in army barracks in el Da'ien, the Quwait al Salaam began training local Arab youths who were then sent to join the Popular Defence Forces in Dar Masalit. A number of local Arab militia leaders, among them Abdalla Abu Shineibat and Omar Babboush, a Miseriya omda, began receiving money from the government for the first time.[25]

During al Dabi's sojourn in Dar Masalit, the PDF began rejecting non-Arab recruits and getting itself a name, among Masalit, as 'Janjawiid'. The confusion between the official government militia (PDF) and unofficial militias (Janjawiid) was so complete that many Masalit believed the entire PDF had been replaced by Janjawiid. In 2004, the SLA commander of Dar Masalit would say that 'things changed in 1999. The PDF ended and the Janjawiid came. The Janjawiid occupied all PDF places.' More than thirty villages were burned and more than 1,000 Masalit killed in the three months al Dabi spent in Geneina.[26] Governor Yahya complained to Dabi, and asked: 'Why us? We are not SPLA.' Dabi responded: 'I have orders from the government. All our orders come from the government. We are here so no-one can point a finger at the government.'[27]

Al Dabi had good contacts with Libya – he had visited Tripoli in June 1989, reportedly to organize arms supplies – and government-backed militia forces killed in the Masalit war included non-Sudanese Arabs, Libyans and Chadians. Many of the *Janjawiid* leaders who emerged in West Darfur in al Dabi's time were of recent Chadian origin. The families of Babboush and Shineibat had come to Darfur from Chad. Another *Janjawiid* leader, Omda Saef, belonged to the Awlad Zeid section of the Mahamid which initially came from Chad to rear the herds of the Masalit Sultan.

Then there was Musa Hilal, whose men were already active even in West Darfur and already accountable, apparently, only to Khartoum. In 2000, Mohamed Basher, currently a senior official in the Justice and Equality Movement, was a city councillor in Geneina. He came across permits signed by Musa Hilal to authorize the carriage of weapons without let or hindrance. Basher complained to the governor, Omar Haroun, and was told: 'We can't do anything. We will send your complaint to Khartoum.'

From Aamo to Misteriha

Colonel Gaddafi had been mentor of the Arab Gathering. When relations with the Arab League soured in the 1990s, he turned his attention towards building strategic alliances in Africa, and opened Libya's borders to African workers. But about one-third of Libya's youth were unemployed, and race riots in 2000 killed an estimated 250 black migrants. Thousands more were expelled from the country. Many African Arabs who had been in Libya under the umbrella of the Arab Gathering, more a meeting of minds then than a structured organization, moved across the border to North Darfur, where they were divided among six camps.[28] A visitor to the camps in 2000 found military trainers from Yasser Arafat's Palestine Liberation Organization. He also found Musa Hilal controlling two of the camps, close to Kebkabiya.

By 1992, Musa Hilal was already a key figure in the Arab Gathering in Darfur. In November of that year, he represented the Um Jalul at a meeting organized by leaders of the Arab Gathering with the intention of making a permanent Arab settlement at Rahad Gineid, the place where his father's kinsmen had fought the Zaghawa in the 1960s and where Arab herders had killed fifteen Zaghawa in a bloody fight over access in 1991.[29] The 1992 meeting, at Rahad Gineid itself, was a failure. Zaghawa militants got wind of it and forced the regional government, under threat of attack, to agree 'not to violate any traditional rights or to establish new rights' in the area.[30]

The next flashpoint for Rizeigat–Zaghawa conflict was the Abu Gamra area. Abubaker Hamid Nur was there.

> I saw many Arabs from Chad. They had travelled more than
> 250 miles I asked why, and they said, 'We are from Chad, but
> our roots are here.' What was very strange was that they had
> weapons and government soldiers were near. I told the govern-
> ment, 'Foreigners have weapons.' The reply was, 'These are
> orders from Khartoum. Do not intervene.'[31]

Another hotspot was Aamo – known as Dawa to the Zaghawa. Checkpoints were erected, travellers stopped and searched, and luggage stolen. In 1994, two trucks carrying twenty-seven Zaghawa travelling north from Kutum were intercepted at night and burned. Seventeen Zaghawa were killed.[32] For Musa Hilal, war was not a continuation of politics by other means; it was the only means he knew. When members of the Um Jalul came under suspicion in 1996 of stealing camels from the Zaghawa people of Donky al Hosh, a water point on the Gineid route, Musa Hilal reacted violently. The local sheikh, Dili Ahmad, had initially welcomed the Um Jalul and now approached his Um Jalul counterpart, Musa Hilal, with a view to discussing the problem. Hilal responded by attacking Sheikh Ahmad's people. The feud took dozens of lives in the following weeks and months.[33]

In 1996 Musa Hilal settled in Misteriha, on land occupied by the Um Jalul's Ereigat cousins. They, too, were active in the Arab Gathering through General Abdalla Safi al Nur, the most influential Abbala Rizeigat in Khartoum, who, according to friends, played an important role in convincing the government that Arabs could achieve great things in Darfur – if only they had backing. Government support for Musa Hilal's Janjawiid changed qualitatively when Safi al Nur was made governor of North Darfur in January 2000, just as the Bashir–Turabi split gave Khartoum good reason to fear a new opposition front emerging in Darfur. It was during Safi al Nur's fourteen-month governorship that helicopters began arriving in Misteriha and the Zaghawa stopped selling their camels there.[34] Weapons were collected from non-Arabs, even in the police force, and given to Hilal's men. New PDF leaders were brought in, mostly drawn from Misteriha and other Abbala Rizeigat settlements.

With grassroots Darfurian opposition growing and Darfurian Islamists abandoning the ruling party in droves, senior figures in regional and central government accelerated the mobilization of Darfur's Abbala Arabs. The key players were three Ereigat: Abdalla Safi al Nur; General Hussein Abdalla Jibril, an MP and chairman of the Parliamentary Security and Defence Committee; and Jibril Abdalla, minister of education in the North Darfur government. In South Darfur, among the most active were Lt. Gen. Adam Hamid Musa, a Zayadiya Arab and future governor of South Darfur state, and three Baggara Rizeigat – Abdel Hamid Musa Kasha, minister of foreign trade in the Khartoum government; Abdalla Ali Masar, governor of River Nile state and a prime mover of the 1987 Arab

Gathering letter to Sadiq al Mahdi; and Hasabo Abdel Rahman, a senior security officer.[35] Musa Hilal was, increasingly, their muscle, helped at the national level with arms and ammunition from Khartoum and at the local level with vehicles 'loaned' from the Jebel Marra development project.

After 2001, as Fur and Zaghawa militants began organizing what would soon become the Sudan Liberation Army, government and Janjawiid leaders sought help from other countries – including Chad, Nigeria, Cameroon, the Central African Republic, Senegal, Niger and Mali. Safi al Nur and Musa Hilal visited Chad, promising volunteers money, a horse, a gun and loot without limit. Some 20,000 reportedly accepted the offer, among them the remnants of the Um Bakha militia – 'bakha' referring to the plastic water containers that they beat and rattled to terrify the villages they raided – and others who went by the names Um Kwak and Janjawiid. These volunteers were spread among four Janjawiid camps equipped and trained by the government. Misteriha, in North Darfur, was for the Abbala Rizeigat. South Darfur had two camps – Jebel Adola for southern Rizeigat and Ma'aliya, and Gardud for Sa'ada and Baggara Beni Halba. West Darfur had one – Jebel Kargo in Wadi Saleh for Terjem, Ta'aisha and Salamat.[36]

In October 2002, government-supported Janjawiid from the camps in South Darfur launched a major offensive, the first of its kind against Fur civilians. They would sweep down on a village before dawn. Men were killed and often mutilated, women raped, and children sometimes abducted. Villages were burnt, livestock seized, fields torched, and all infrastructure methodically destroyed. By the beginning of 2003, at least 160 civilians had been killed, hundreds more wounded and hundreds of villages burned.[37] Tens of thousands had fled the land, often seeking safety high in Jebel Marra. It was a prelude to the firestorm that would soon sweep all across Darfur.

During that critical year, 2002, it became clear that the Janjawiid enjoyed complete impunity. In the words of a tribal leader in Dar

Zaghawa who was once not unfriendly to the government: 'When the Janjawiid burned a village, our people went to the police, but the government didn't care about it. But if Zaghawa attacked Arabs, they went quickly to kill the Zaghawa.' Worse even than impunity, people suspected that powerful men in government in Khartoum were giving the orders. Determination to resist was growing.

4

The Rebels

He was, at first acquaintance, an unlikely rebel – a security officer, briefly, in the Nimeiri regime who had travelled across the Arab world for eight years, more concerned with making money than with the NIF's seizure of power back in Sudan. But on returning to Sudan in 1994, Khamis Abakir soon had a first brush with NIF law: angered by the state's refusal to release money he had made while working abroad, he demonstrated publicly in the streets of Khartoum, and spent two days in jail.[1] A decade later, he was the SLA's most prominent Masalit commander, surrounded by a vastly disparate group of men like him – men who were not political animals, but who knew injustice when they saw it and who, after years of rising conflict with the government and government-backed militias, finally felt they had nothing left to lose. They, like him, were Muslims; most, unlike him, were devout Muslims who prayed five times a day – on the sand beside their horses if on patrol or, if camped, under the mango trees where they slept. They ranged from teenagers in second-hand T-shirts to 50-year-old men with gnarled peasants' hands. Their courtesy was striking: without being asked, they fetched water for washing and drinking, offered the best bits of meat on the rare occasions

Khamis Abakir, SLA commander, 2004

that they had meat, and walked willingly for hours to gather information about this village or that.

These were not the 'armed bandits' the government insisted they were. They were farmers who had been driven from their smallholdings by men wearing army uniforms. Their attacks so far had been precise, against military and security targets. Some had served in the police or army, turning a blind eye to ethnic discrimination until the government they served began attacking their villages and killing their families.

Khamis Ahmad Osman had spent twenty-one years in the army. He encountered discrimination from the outset. Arabs got two holidays a year; non-Arabs only one. Arab friends who had signed on with him became officers; he never rose above sergeant. He accepted this without protest, seeing no other route out of poverty, until his village, Kassieh, was burned and twenty-one people including his brother, the village imam, were killed. At this point, he asked himself: 'Why am I working for the government? I am not working for money. I am working for my community.'[2] He joined the SLA as soon as he heard of it, to fight 'for freedom and justice'. The Masalit had never had hospitals or schools, he said. Now they had been driven off their land. They had nothing.

Ali Yaqub Idriss, always impeccable in a blue shirt with two pens in the pocket, had spent twelve years in the police force.

> Arabs pass examinations; Africans do not. My Arab friends
> became officers; I did not. Arab police are kept in the towns.
> African police are sent to villages, where salaries come late. If
> you go to the town to protest you are told: 'Who ordered you
> to come here? Go back!'

In 1999, Idriss had been jailed for three months for criticizing the mistreatment of civilians. 'Arab police beat any African who is accused. They torture them by pulling them along with strips of rubber tyre around their necks. Investigations are always done by Arab police. You know the results...' He joined the SLA after his village, Nouri Jebel, was attacked in December 2003. Almost fifty villagers were killed, and he could name them all. 'It is the Janjawiid who are criminals – not us', he said on a journey through the burned villages of Dar Masalit. 'I was a policeman. I know them all. Many have been in jail, but bought their release. Ali Ibrahim, thief! Brema Labid, thief! Shineibat, thief! Hamid Dawai, thief!'

There was a smattering of professionals, too, among Abakir's men. Jamal Abdel Hamman gave up his job in a Khartoum law firm and returned to work as a teacher in his home village, Abun, after four relatives were killed when government planes bombed the town of Habila in August 2003. He joined the SLA after government and Janjawiid forces burned Abun to the ground in February 2004. Mohamed Dafa'alla had been a doctor, but joined the rebels, and put hand grenades in his pockets, after Janjawiid burned his clinic in Dreisa.

Like most early rebel commanders, Abakir came to the SLA through the self-defence groups which first emerged in Fur areas

Branch : Max Webber
Phone : 02 9839 6677
Date   : 7/09/2018   Time: 2:26 PM
Name   : OKELLO, LAZARUS

ITEM(S) BORROWED   DUE DATE

Darfur : a short history of.. 28 Sep 2018

We're online at
www.libraries.blacktown.nsw.gov.au

Thank you for using
Blacktown City Libraries.

You can leave reviews for library items
via our online catalogue.
blacktown.spydus.com

in reponse to conflict in the mid-1980s. His return to Darfur in
1995 had coincided with the administrative reorganization of West
Darfur, which Masalit saw as an attempt to usurp the authority of
their sultan. They reacted angrily and communal hostilities broke
out. In August 1995, heavily armed Arab raiders stole 40,000
head of cattle and drove them east towards Zalingei, burning the
village of Mejmeri on the way and killing twenty-three civilians.
It was a massacre without precedent, but the state government
did nothing. In June 1996, another threshold was passed when
raiders burned seven villages – Shushta, Kassim Beli, Haraza,
Awir Radu, Deeta, Sisi and Torre – in a single day. Thirteen men
and five women, one of whom was pregnant, were killed; two
others were thrown into a flaming hut and burned alive.[3] Again
the government failed to react. Abakir began rallying Masalit
youths, telling them this was not a little local trouble with Arab
pastoralists but a government plan to change the ethnic geography
of the region. They began to form self-defence groups, to defend
their families and their farms.

As the conflict escalated, government soldiers were seen training Arab irregulars in Jebel Endia, north of Geneina. Setting out
from Jebel Endia, these irregulars – primarily Beni Halba, Maharia
and Um Jalul – burned all villages north and west of Geneina,
meeting little resistance. Abakir moved to the offensive and in
December 1997 led 130 men to Jebel Endia. Most were farmers
who had to sell camels to buy weapons. But they defeated the
government in a six-hour battle that ended when the government
forces fled to Chad, ten miles away, leaving seven men dead.
Abakir lost none of his men.

After this, he said, the burning became continuous.[4] 'They
began burning villages twice. By the end of 1998, more than
100,000 Masalit had fled to Chad. We had no choice but to
organize. We were fighting for our lives.'

In May 1999, Abakir was captured in his home village of
Fanganta, a stone's throw from the Chad border. He was sentenced

to twenty years' imprisonment for armed rebellion, but escaped after five years. For four of those years he was held in solitary confinement in tiny, windowless cells, shackled and regularly beaten. Despite this, his vision was of a future where Arab and non-Arab would live together as before. 'Our problem is not with the Arabs', he said. 'It is with the government.'

The Fur Resistance

As Abakir began to organize self-defence units in Dar Masalit in 1996, and presidential elections gave a veneer of respectability to the NIF's seizure of power, a meeting took place in Khartoum which contained the seeds of the future rebel movement in Darfur. The meeting brought together three young Fur activists – Abdel Wahid Mohamed al Nur, a lawyer and the SLA's first chairman, Ahmad Abdel Shafi, an education student and the SLA's first co-ordinator; and Abdu Abdalla Ismail, a modern languages graduate and the SLA's first representative in the Ceasefire Commission headquarters set up under the African Union in al Fasher. The three had little political experience, but they established a clandestine organization of remarkable effectiveness.

'We had heard about looting and burning and knew that the Arab Gathering was working very hard, arming Arab tribes and training them in the PDF', Abdel Shafi recalled almost a decade later.[5]

> Its publications said: 'We are going to kill all zurga [blacks]. Darfur is now Dar al Arab.' They were trying to force us to leave, to take over water and grazing. We said: 'The government is planning to crush our people. What can we do?' We spoke to members of parliament in Khartoum. They agreed on the threat, but said: 'What can we do about it?' We began talking about rebellion and started collecting money from our people in Khartoum.

With the money raised in Khartoum – more than a million Sudanese pounds, an unexpectedly large sum – the Fur bought ammunition from kinsmen in the army and distributed it among self-defence groups. Babikir Abdalla, a young lawyer working in Qatar, began fund-raising among expatriates.

Soon the Fur decided to try to organize the scattered resistance activities that were emerging all over Darfur, starting from the mountainous stronghold of Jebel Marra. Babikir returned from Qatar and Abdel Wahid from Syria, and in October 1997 they met Abdel Shafi in Jebel Marra, set on winning the support of the *akadas*, the village commanders who led Fur self-defence groups. Their message to the *akadas* was that the real enemy was not the Arabs; it was the government. Young men should be encouraged not to leave Jebel Marra in search of work or education, but to stay in their villages, where they would be trained.

Training on this scale needed serious money, and Abdel Shafi and Babikir travelled to Chad to seek help from President Idriss Deby. They were, they admit, political innocents: Chad and Sudan had signed a mutual security agreement and Deby refused even to meet them. With only $100 between them, the pair soon found themselves without a penny in their pockets and were forced to sell clothes and blankets to fund their way back to Jebel Marra. But they were not discouraged and on their return to Darfur their message was unequivocal: 'The Arabs will not allow us to stay in our land unless we defend ourselves. It is a war of "to be or not to be."' Army veterans were brought in to train new recruits. Each household was asked to provide a little millet for the recruits and emergency food reserves were sold to buy ammunition. Sheikhs saw their powers whittled away as the activists argued that *akadas* carried greater authority in time of war. By December 1997, the whole of Jebel Marra was mobilized and Abdel Wahid began organizing armed groups outside the mountains, in Zalingei and Wadi Saleh. Abdel Shafi returned to Khartoum to mobilize students, political leaders and women. In the evenings he toured the suburbs, asking for financial contributions to help defend Darfur.

In 2000, seizing the opportunity of the split in the ruling party, Fur in Khartoum set up 'cultural groups' that provided a front for political activity and fund-raising. The Ali Dinar Centre for Education and Culture was established, ostensibly to raise awareness about the history and culture of the Fur, in Khartoum's suburbs and shanty towns – Mayo, Haj Yousif and Soba – and soon after in the eastern Sudanese towns of Gedaref and New Halfa where many Fur had migrated in search of work. A young law student, Tayyib Bashar, was mandated to mobilize students to return to Darfur and formed the Darfur Students' Union. In Jebel Marra, military camps were established outside villages for the first time. To support the new activities, Fur professionals and those in government service were asked to pay a small monthly tax.

From the very beginning, Abdel Wahid and his group sought to situate the Fur struggle in a wider context, believing that only unity could defeat the NIF. Their first overture, in 1999, was to the Masalit, a tribe with which they shared a common border and which, like them, had suffered for many years at the hands of government-backed militias.[6] But the Masalit were hesitant to take action that might exacerbate their suffering. They had bitter recent experience of how any action, however small, could escalate. On 17 January 1999, al Haj Ismail Ishaq Omar, an elderly Masalit farmer from the village of Tabarik, had found animals belonging to Arab herders trampling his fields. When he attempted to chase the animals away, the herders shot and killed him and three other villagers. In the ensuing confrontation, two Arabs were killed, one of them a chief who was trying to restore calm. In Khartoum, Interior Minister Abdel Rahim Mohamed Hussein announced that the Masalit had assassinated all Arab leaders in Dar Masalit and declared that they were outlaws, a fifth column in league with the SPLA. Government troops sealed off Dar Masalit as militias backed by government helicopters launched a series of attacks that killed more than two thousand people.[7]

The Fur decided to remain in contact with Masalit activists, but not to identify themselves as a political movement, even to their own people. Abdel Shafi attempted, but failed, to make contact with the SPLA underground cells in Khartoum.

The Zaghawa Link

It was not until 2001 that the Fur forged their first alliance – not with the Masalit, with whom they had so much in common, but with the Zaghawa. Like the Fur, the Zaghawa leadership had arrived at the point of armed rebellion late and reluctantly. Within Darfur, the Zaghawa had clashed with both Arabs and Fur, but had most often been aligned with Arabs – Chadian and Darfurian. The early architects of the Arab Gathering had identified them as a potential constituency. In the 1980s, a Sudanese Zaghawa named Abdalla Zakaria Idriss was one of the main implementers of Libya's plans in Chad and Darfur. In the 1990s, the Zaghawa were well represented in the NIF.

The drought of the 1980s brought a sea change. As competition for precious water sources increased, the Zaghawa began establishing small armed camps across their homeland in the months when Arab herders moved north to water their animals. In 1987 the pattern was reversed: drought in North Darfur drove Zaghawa south, where they were attacked, south of Kebkabiya, by Arab militias. Dozens of Zaghawa were killed in the fighting and the survivors were chased back north. By the time the chase was over, almost 200 people were dead.[8] A peace meeting of tribal elders in Kutum reached agreement on compensation, but the agreement was not honoured. The Qoreish manifestos kindled fears. 'We knew trouble was coming when we saw the letters of the Arab Gathering', said Omda Bakhit Dabo Hashem of Furawiya.

Zaghawa SLA forces

'We heard of the burning of Dar Fur and saw it from Nyala. The attackers wrote *Tahrir Watan al Arabi* – The Liberated Arab Nation – in the ashes. Then there was the administrative reorganization of Dar Masalit – and the camels began eating our gardens.' Young Zaghawa activists began buying weapons. Intermittent clashes continued, with half-hearted efforts by the government and tribal leaders to mediate. In May 1991, Zaghawa elders sent a memorandum to President Bashir, complaining that the government was creating an 'apartheid region' in Darfur by instigating 'crimes against humanity', manipulating tribal hierarchies for political ends and attempting to turn 'black' tribes against each other.[9] In 1997, a second conference in Kutum agreed that Arab herders would be permitted to move on specific routes, escorted by government forces. But once again the agreement was not enforced, and in 1998 six of the seasonal camps that young Zaghawa herders had established more than a decade earlier became permanent armed camps.

After government troops and Janjawiid killed fifty-seven Zaghawa in the Mershing area, between al Fasher and Nyala, the young Turks felt it was time to strike back, but found that most Zaghawa disagreed. Despite this, activists began recruiting, here and there, and made off with a car and some horses in a first attack on a police station near Abu Gamra. They began putting down roots in Ain Moro and Ain Sirro, west of Fata Borno and Kutum, seeing traditional mediation wholly unequipped to prevent Janjawiid from moving with impunity all across North Darfur, attacking civilians, rustling animals, kidnapping and killing on the roads. In 1999, tribal leaders met with senior government officials in Khartoum, but in doing so exacerbated tension. The young activists complained that 'the *omdas* took money from the government and didn't stop the war.'[10]

In 2001, Zaghawa began to refuse to pay taxes to a government that 'provided no security at all for human beings in Dar Zaghawa, no medical services and no education system.'[11] Attacks escalated. A Janjawiid offensive killed 125 civilians in Abu Gamra before sweeping east. For the Zaghawa, this offensive marked a turning point. The dead of Abu Gamra included thirty-six villagers who had been meeting to try to reopen local schools. Among them were two head teachers – al Nur Musa Issa, 45, head of Abu Gamra girls' primary school, and Ali Mohamed Suleiman, 43, head of the parallel boys' school.[12] Zaghawa outside Darfur – expatriates in Libya, merchants and students in Khartoum – now agreed that there was a need to form an organized resistance group similar to the one they were hearing of in Jebel Marra. Daud Taher Hariga, a Zaghawa businessman who had been documenting the Fur conflict since the early 1980s, was asked to accompany Abdel Wahid Mohamed al Nur to Jebel Marra to visit the camps the Fur were organizing.

The two men left from Khartoum on 1 July 2001, bound first for Geneina, where they hoped, but failed, to meet leaders of the Masalit resistance. From Jebel Marra, they travelled to North

Darfur. After a second attempt to meet Masalit representatives in Kebkabiya, they arrived in the town of Kornoi on 20 July and met immediately with the committee that had been formed to manage the Zaghawa camps.[13] The committee agreed to joint efforts with the Fur and gave Daud Taher a mandate to speak for the Zaghawa.

When Did the Insurrection Begin?

It is usually said that the rebellion in Darfur began on 26 February 2003 when a group calling itself the Darfur Liberation Front (DLF) issued a statement claiming an attack on Golo, the district headquarters of Jebel Marra. But by the time of the attack on Golo, war was already raging in Darfur: the rebels were attacking police stations, army posts and convoys, and Jebel Marra was under massive air and ground attack. The international community was slow to notice the rebellion in Darfur, focused as it was on efforts to end the war in Southern Sudan. But the existence of a rebel movement in Darfur had been known to the government since an attack on a police station in Golo in June 2002.[14]

Although it is difficult to identify a single date for the beginning of the rebellion, given the SLA's slow emergence from similar but separate tribally based movements, the most precise is 21 July 2001, when an expanded Fur and Zaghawa group met in Abu Gamra and swore a solemn oath on the Quran to work together to foil Arab supremacist policies in Darfur. On the Fur side, the group included Abdel Wahid and Abdu Ismail. On the Zaghawa side, it included the first three military leaders of the future rebel movement – Khater Tor al Khalla, Abdalla Abakir and Jumaa Mohamed Hagar. The Zaghawa all belonged to the Tuer branch of the tribe, which, although Sudanese, supported Idriss Deby in his bid to overthrow Hissène Habré in 1990. Deby had used Tuer territory as his rear base, and fought his way to N'Djamena with Tuer at his side. On finding no payback there, they had returned to Darfur, temporarily rebels without a cause.

The two groups decided to continue efforts to forge an alliance with Masalit activists, and finally succeeded at a meeting in Zalingei in November 2001. They agreed not to declare themselves as a movement until they had strong political and logistical support, which they estimated would take at least twelve months. Most importantly, they agreed to send 150 Zaghawa for training in Jebel Marra. A first group of seventeen left the same day, led by Khater Tor al Khalla.

The plan called for the Zaghawa to stay in Jebel Marra for only three weeks. But many stayed on when training ended, and on 25 February 2002 they mounted a first joint operation against a garrison in the south of the mountain, between Nyala and Tur.[15] Like the SPLA in its day, the SLA began its military activities before its political agenda was clarified. But the operation was a success: the garrison was burned, arms seized and the government troops routed.

The head of security in Khartoum, Major General Salah Abdalla 'Gosh', was alarmed. The Fur–Zaghawa alliance and the military proficiency of the rebels were disturbing. In the National Assembly, an Ereigat Arab MP from North Darfur, Hussein Abdalla Jibril, called for action. Jibril complained that 'the Fur are arming themselves! Instead of growing mangoes they are growing hashish!' Mohamed Baraka, a Fur MP from Kebkabiya, whose village of Shoba had already been attacked more than a dozen times, replied, 'Why do we not discuss the Janjawiid attacks on Jebel Marra?' He protested that the 300 army soldiers in Kebkabiya, just five miles from Shoba, had never moved to protect his village. Seventeen Fur MPs signed the petition demanding a debate. To their surprise, President Bashir invited them to present their case.

By the time the Fur MPs went to Bashir's home on 1 May, the war had escalated. Their petition documented 181 attacks on

83 villages in Kebkabiya, Jebel Marra, Zalingei and Kas. A total of 420 people had been killed and thousands of animals stolen. At least two of the villages – Danga and Tambasi – had begun to be settled by Arabs and had been given Arab names – Um al Gura and Um Dawan-Ban. This was the first real publicity for the growing conflict in Darfur, and the security chiefs were angry. Bashir formed a committee, for the 'Restoration of State Authority and Security in Darfur', chaired by General Ibrahim Suleiman. Its first act, following the attack on Golo, was to detain activists on both sides, including two dozen Arab militants and sixty-six prominent Fur including lawyers, teachers and elders. Some of the Fur were accused of belonging to a group called the Darfur Liberation Front.[16] One of these, arrested in Zalingei on 11 July, was Abdel Wahid Mohamed al Nur.

Four weeks after his arrest, Abdel Wahid wrote a letter from jail that was smuggled outside Sudan. It shed some light on the hidden conflict in Darfur and brought him to international attention for the first time. 'In the area of Jebel Marra, Zalingei and Kebkabiya', he wrote, 'the security forces act with virtual immunity, terrorizing the Fur people, raiding houses randomly, arresting people including the elderly and children, and detaining them without charge or trial. Many Fur men have fled to the mountains, to find a safe haven, and have left their lands.' He spoke of the suffering of prisoners held under emergency legislation without charge or trial: 'The cell space is 16 square metres and is overcrowded: there are twelve of us in this small room without ventilation or windows.'

Security's calculation was that, with the leadership decapitated, the embryonic rebel movement would wither and die. It was wrong. Attacks on government forces continued. After an army bus was ambushed on the road between Zalingei and Nyala, and three soldiers were killed, the government agreed to let Fur MPs and chiefs assemble in the small town of Nyertete, on the eastern flank of Jebel Marra, to 'solve the Fur problem', and released a number of Fur detainees to attend it – though not Abdel Wahid. It was the government's second miscalculation.

On 16 August 2002, the 'Fur Leadership Conference' opened in Nyertete, attended by 129 delegates and chaired by Sultan Hussein Ayoub Ali. The delegates' first act was not what the government wanted: they sent ten men up the mountain to find out the rebels' demands. Mohamed Baraka was one of them.[17] A few miles outside Nyertete, in an area completely controlled by the rebels, Baraka found a large meeting in progress between the DLF and the local people, with banners in the Fur language. In front of the crowd, a DLF leader, Abdalla Abakir, presented ambitious demands. The ten reported back to Nyertete, where the consensus was that the DLF was asking for too much. It would be better to meet alone with the leaders and discuss their real needs. So the ten men trekked back up the mountain and sat until the early hours of the morning with Abakir and his fellow commanders. There were just twenty-three armed men in the main rebel camp, and they were ready to withdraw from Jebel Marra. They wanted medicines for their wounded, and a month to prepare.

In a closing statement on 22 August, notable for its conciliatory tone and criticism of all armed actions, the Leadership Conference avoided pointing a finger at 'Arabs' and put the blame for the trouble in Jebel Marra squarely on the government's shoulders. It said Khartoum had failed to implement previous agreements. It had also failed, 'with all its instruments', to tackle injustices and grievances. The government's own forces had committed 'many wrong acts', including rape, and 'continuous humiliation' of Fur civilians. If there was support for rebels, it was because the people had lost all confidence in the security forces. The conference demanded that 'the state carry out its duties in a decisive and firm way to stop the repeated aggressions carried out by some Arab tribes (*Janjawiid*) against the land and possessions of the Fur'. But the conference also condemned attacks against the police and, stressing the need to maintain Fur unity, sent a thinly veiled warning to the rebels. 'No individual or group has the right to decide any affairs of the tribe without being delegated.' It called for the release of all detainees, the implementation of previous agreements and the withdrawal from Jebel Marra of all 'foreign forces'.

The Nyertete Conference was a brave attempt, very late in the day, at compromise by the Fur leaders. But the alliance between Security and the Arab Gathering killed it. Less than a month later, another conference was convened in Kas, thirty miles to the south, under the auspices of a well-known supporter of Arab Gathering ideology – Maj. Gen. Salah Ali al Ghali, governor of South Darfur. Although billed as the 'Conference of Peaceful Co-existence for the Tribes in and around Jebel Marra', the Kas conference blamed all the trouble in the region on Fur militias, supported, it said, by the Popular Police and Popular Defence Forces. It demanded a 'decisive step' against the militias and the 'liquidation of the PDF'. It demanded the creation of additional 'nomad constituencies' and development programmes for 'nomads', completely ignoring the rehabilitation needed in Fur areas. It called for the release of local leaders arrested in North Darfur – among them, a month earlier, Musa Hilal.

Most Fur perceived the Kas conference as a rejection of the resolutions reached in Nyertete, even as 'a declaration of war' on the Fur. And not without reason. Even as it was claiming to be seeking peace, Khartoum was attempting to win the active support of Arab tribes in the region. Government officials approached the *nazir* of the Beni Halba, el Hadi Issa Dabaka, and offered him a car, furniture, money and precious development projects if he would throw his tribe behind the *Janjawiid*. The *nazir* had despatched his *fursan* militia against the SPLA in 1991, but this time he refused, saying: 'If an enemy attacks me on my own land, I will defend myself.'[18]

By the beginning of 2003, Jebel Marra was surrounded by government forces. It was under attack from government-supported militias that had already made two attempts to root out the rebels and from Antonov bombers and helicopter gunships that were bombing indiscriminately. One exile group reported that more than a hundred Fur civilians were killed between October 2002 and the year's end.[19]

Looking for Friends

For political and logistical support, the Fur and Zaghawa rebels looked initially to the Sudan Federal Democratic Alliance of Ahmed Diraige, the former governor now in exile and prominent in the opposition National Democratic Alliance. They found sympathy from his deputy, Sharif Harir, who had resigned his post as a lecturer in social anthropology in Norway in 1995 and gone to Eritrea to head the SFDA forces based there. Harir initially claimed the fighters in Jebel Marra were the military wing of the SFDA. But Diraige disagreed with him over the wisdom of armed rebellion and the DLF got no practical help from the SFDA. Some within the SLA say it was at this point that the SPLA leader, John Garang, offered Abdel Wahid support – on condition that he stopped looking to the SFDA, and looked south instead.

The nature and extent of the relationship between the SLA and the SPLA was, from the very beginning, a matter of heated debate, both inside and outside the SLA. The Sudan government claimed that Abdel Wahid was being supplied by the SPLA and attempted to depict the rebels as tools of the Southerners. The SLA denied, and continues to deny, any links save ideological sympathy. SLA leaders say their first official contact with the SPLA came in January 2003, when Ahmad Abdel Shafi and Babikir Abdalla succeeded in catching Garang at Nairobi airport as he waited for a flight to Nigeria. At a second meeting on his return from Nigeria, Garang urged the Fur to organize militarily and politically and to publish a manifesto.[20] 'Without strong political work', he told them, 'the government will call you thieves and robbers.'

When the Darfur rebels attacked and briefly occupied Golo the following month, they attempted, for the first time, to set up a rebel-led civilian administration. The man chosen as administrator, Abdalla Korah, appealed to local people to support him to end the marginalization and injustice that he said was depriving Darfur of development.[21] It was the first political statement by the rebels that reached the outside world. Days later, Abdel Wahid announced, in telephone calls to Sudanese researchers in London, that the Darfur rebels were concerned with the rights of all marginalized Sudanese. To reflect this, he said, the DLF had been renamed the Sudan Liberation Army/Movement, or SLA/SLM. The change was the first evidence of intensive talks between SLA leaders and an SPLA team that included Abdel Aziz Adam al Hilu, commander of the Nuba Mountains, and Malik Agar, commander of Southern Blue Nile.[22] The talks covered a range of issues – logistics, political orientation and, most critically in the SPLA's view, the absolute imperative of maintaining unity. The SPLA argued that the Darfurians should not join the Naivasha process. First, they should fight – advised by a senior SPLA commander who was sent to Darfur to coordinate with them.

Two months after meeting Garang, on 16 March 2003, the SLA/M made public its 'Political Declaration', or manifesto. The declaration bears a striking resemblance to the SPLA's vision of a united 'New Sudan', demanding 'a New Sudan that belongs equally to all its citizens', and senior SPLA members admit that they co-authored it. Like the SPLA, the SLA deplored political and economic marginalization and demanded decentralization and the right of self-determination as a basis for 'viable' unity. Like the SPLA, it demanded secular government. Without specifically mentioning Sharia law, it said: 'Religion belongs to the individual and the state belongs to all of us.' It appealed to Arabs to join it:

> The Arab tribes and groups are an integral and indivisible
> component of Darfur social fabric who have been equally

marginalized and deprived of their rights to development and genuine political participation.... The real interests of the Arab tribes of Darfur are with the SLM/A and Darfur not with the various oppressive and transient governments of Khartoum.

Four days later, the SPLA issued a declaration of its own.[23] It denied any connection to the 'inception' of the war in Darfur but expressed 'full political solidarity with the people of Darfur and their just cause'. It said agreement being hammered out in the North–South peace talks in Naivasha on the status of the so-called Three Areas – the Nuba Mountains, Abyei and Blue Nile – could be the 'correct formula' for Darfur too.

In fact the SPLA had tried to organize Darfur resistance some years earlier. In the late 1990s, as the Arab–Masalit conflict escalated, a young Masalit activist called Adam Bazooka had travelled to Eritrea to seek help in organizing a Masalit self-defence force from the commander of SPLA's 'New Sudan Brigade' – Adam Aziz al Hilu. Mostly Masalit migrants in eastern Sudan began crossing the border to Eritrea, where hundreds were trained and armed by the SPLA. In 2001, these troops were transferred to Raja in Bahr el Ghazal and formed part of an offensive to open a new front in Darfur. Blocked before reaching Darfur, the SPLA's force drained away and many Masalit returned to their homes, to reappear in the ranks of the SLA two years later.

The issue of relations with the SPLA was soon to become one of the most divisive issues within an already fractious rebel movement. By late 2004, some Zaghawa commanders were threatening to go their own way if the SLA allowed itself to be 'used' by the SPLA. 'John Garang is a very bad man', said a Zaghawa commander who attended peace talks with the government in Abuja.[24] 'He sent weapons separately to the Fur, Masalit and Zaghawa in order to divide and rule. He wants us to belong to him like Abyei and the Nuba mountains. He wants us to join the Naivasha process. We are going to tell Abdel Wahid we don't want to belong to

the SPLA. The fighters on the ground in Darfur are Zaghawa. They
control all of North Darfur and half of South Darfur. Most SLA
commanders are Zaghawa; most victories are Zaghawa victories.
In the SLA there is no victory without our people.'

SLA officials independent of both main centres of power within
the SLA – commanders grouped around Abdel Wahid, and others
loyal to the SLA's self-styled secretary general, Minni Arkoy Minawi
– acknowledge that weapons were sent to the SLA: first to Jebel
Marra and then, when Jebel Marra came under heavy attack, to
Dar Zaghawa.[25] But they say the shipments originated in Eritrea
and were only passed on by the SPLA, and their destination was
determined by security considerations rather than any attempt
by the SPLA to divide and rule. Subsequent deliveries to Jebel
Marra, after punitive infighting in the middle of 2004 between
the partisans of Abdel Wahid and Zaghawa supporters of Minni
Minawi, may have been designed to shore up the Fur. This is
certainly the view of most Zaghawa.

The Eritreans were both consistent and opportunistic. As early
as 1995, as part of his efforts to punish Sudan for destabilizing
Eritrea, President Isseyas Afewerki had sent a secret mission to
N'Djamena to try to persuade Deby to help open a 'western front'
against Khartoum. The mission got nowhere: Deby did not want
to anger the Sudanese security officers who had helped him to
power and who were still present in force in Chad. Thereafter,
Eritrea had reverted to supporting SPLA and Beja guerrillas based
on its own territory, along Sudan's eastern border. But Afewerki
persisted in believing that President Bashir should be overthrown
by force, and gave arms to any group ready to do that.

Whatever John Garang's designs on the SLA, criticism of
Abdel Wahid's contacts with the SPLA ignored more fundamental
problems which sprang from ethnic divisions, issues of personal-
ity, the lack of leadership skills and the rapid growth of the
movement, especially after the spectacular attack on al Fasher. In
its early days, the SLA leadership was clandestine and disciplined.

But Darfur was already militarized. The Fur had their *akadas*, the Zaghawa their armed camps and the Masalit their self-defence groups. All had trained army men who had deserted, and the Zaghawa had experts in desert warfare from the Chadian campaigns. There was no way the young SLA leaders could impose their command either on these seasoned warriors with their own guns and followers or on the thousands of raw recruits who flooded the infant movement as a result of triumph but also defeat. From a few hundred recruits in 2001, the SLA had grown, by 2005, to a force of almost 11,000 men organized in thirteen brigades.[26] Many had their own guns, and were driven by bitterness. The SLA emerged into the political arena as a marriage of convenience rather than of conviction – a coming together of tribally organized armed groups on the basis of what united them, with very little discussion of what divided them.

Search for a Cohesive Leadership

In October 2002, at a meeting in the village of Boodkay on the western slopes of Jebel Marra, the emerging movement elected a leadership that divided the top three posts among its three main tribes. Abdel Wahid, a Fur, became chairman; Abdalla Abakir, a Zaghawa, was made chief of staff. The post of deputy chairman was assigned to the Masalit, but was only filled, by Khamis Abakir, in February 2005. Although there were no Arabs in the leadership, several held, or would soon hold, the rank of commander – among them, in southern Darfur, Ahmad Kubbur, a Rizeigat merchant who had been trained by the SPLA; and in eastern Darfur, Ismail Idriss Nawai, a Hawazma Arab lawyer from Kordofan.

The new leadership was soon haunted by the old decision to keep the scope of the movement secret. After the attack on Golo in June 2002, the people of Jebel Marra had welcomed the Zaghawa fighters who were gathering in their areas, believing they were there to help defend Jebel Marra against the Arabs. But when they realized that the rebels were fighting the government, its planes and artillery, they came to see the Zaghawa as a threat. Mistrust between Fur civilians and Zaghawa fighters grew, deepened by memories of inter-tribal fighting in the 1980s and fomented by government agents who spread word that 'the Zaghawa want to expand Dar Zaghawa'. In 2003 it was agreed that most SLA fighters would withdraw towards Dar Zaghawa. But when the time for withdrawal came, many Fur, including Abdel Wahid, remained in Jebel Marra, causing the beginnings of a split along tribal lines.

By 2004, the movement was unrecognizable. The string of victories in the middle months of 2003 had been followed by equally serious defeats marked by the extraordinary viciousness of the government–Janjawiid offensives. Relations between Fur and Zaghawa were stretched to breaking point. When Abdel Wahid found himself surrounded by government forces in the south of Jebel Marra early in 2004, Minni Minawi refused to send reinforcements and the Fur leader had to seek help from the SPLA, which airlifted him and some of his closest aides to Nairobi. A few months later, scores of young rebels died in Jebel Marra in fierce fighting between Fur and Zaghawa – fighting that some Zaghawa said was provoked by an attempt by Minni Minawi to 'reunite' the movement.[27]

The SLA endeavoured to present a united front in its dealings with the international community, especially in peace talks with the Sudan government. But things were very different in the field. As a commander critical of both factions said: 'The troops in Jebel Marra don't get their orders from Jumaa Mohamed, and Dar Zaghawa doesn't hear from Abdel Wahid.'

The first attempt to rebuild SLA unity failed even before it began. Meeting in the Chadian capital, N'Djamena, in April 2004, leaders of the movement agreed to return to Darfur to mend their differences and seal splits. But Abdel Wahid disappeared

– remerging weeks later with a new wife – and Minni Minawi went to Asmara. Instead of building their political cadres, the SLA's leaders became ambassadors. An 'internal–external' divide was added to the ethnic split. Abdel Wahid began to spend all his time outside Darfur, setting up an office in Nairobi and a headquarters in Asmara, and lobbying for international pressure and assistance. Fur leaders who had earlier respected him for taking on the difficult work of organizing the resistance grumbled that he had become a 'hotel guerrilla'. His failure to brief his men in the field on the political developments outside it alienated many of them. Some said they feared that the SLA, under his leadership, would be bullied by John Garang into signing a hasty peace agreement with the Khartoum government – and warned they would not support it.

Another split, equally important for the long-term future of the rebel movement, divided the founder members of the SLA from an older generation who joined the movement in the first flush of its initial military victories. 'The SLA problem is a leadership problem', a commander in his early fifties said late in 2004.[28] 'They are young and inexperienced and leave no openings for intellectuals and men of experience. They have no political system. They are not democratic. They were elected when the SLA had only a few hundred men.' Critics began calling for a conference of commanders and intellectuals, inside Darfur, to revalidate – or renew – the leadership. In February 2005, a group of expatriates added their voices to those inside Darfur. In a statement addressed to the leadership, they accused the leaders of 'trying to deceive the world around them that their movement is united' and said the leadership split was confusing the movement's political vision. 'Adopt a clear structure that has no duality', they said, 'or declare to us that SLM/A is basically two movements or more. The first led by (A), the second by (B) and the third by (C) so the base can choose which one will represent it and the world community can choose which one to deal with.'

In Darfur, in early 2005, some of those most concerned by the disunity within the SLA claimed that hundreds of men were deserting the movement, worried by poor leadership, deteriorating discipline and abusive behaviour by some soldiers and rogue commanders answerable only to themselves. They expressed doubt as to whether the SLA, as presently constituted, could reform itself. 'Be careful', a young Zaghawa graduate warned. 'The SLA does not like criticism.'

The Justice and Equality Movement

The SLA's history is unexplained only because the story has not been told. The origins of the Justice and Equality Movement (JEM) are more controversial. Is JEM a stalking horse for Hassan Turabi, as the government of Sudan claims and many others believe, or a totally independent movement that is 'deeply rooted in all regions', as its chairman, Dr Khalil Ibrahim, maintains?[29]

Hundreds of miles from Darfur, in the Chadian capital N'Djamena, the debate among the men around the coffee table early in 2005 was almost as heated as the fighting across the border. Hassan al Turabi had been a disaster, said one. Under Turabi, the Islamist project in Sudan had foundered in violence and bloodshed. 'We have no reason to destroy our land and people to support Hassan al Turabi. I will not support anything that would take us back to the past.' A failure, agreed a second. Turabi had done nothing for the 'African' people of Darfur – Muslims whose devotion was second to none – even though many had supported him. 'We were marginalized in Turabi's time too. Turabi is nothing.' Only one person disagreed, clearly discomfited by this criticism of the architect of Sudan's Islamic revolution. 'Yes, Turabi took the wrong path', he said. 'But you have to remember that there was a time when people would turn on the radio whenever he was going to speak. Some people started talking the way he talks and smiling the way he smiles. Turabi's problem was that he was too idealistic...'

The interesting thing about this exchange was not that it covered virtually every shade of opinion about the Islamist movement in Sudan, but that the speakers were all senior members of JEM. In the work in progress that is JEM, one thing is indisputable: despite the strong links of some of its leaders to the Islamist movement, and the strong representation of former NIF members who still believe that Islamic values can solve many of Sudan's problems, JEM has attracted Sudanese from across the political spectrum. What unites them, for the moment at least, is anger at the marginalization of regions like Darfur and the failure of all northern politicians, including Turabi, to do anything, ever, about it.

Within the political mix that is JEM there are, however, two main tendencies that dwarf all others. One is tribal, the other Islamic – a sometimes uneasy alliance that could contain the seeds of future division. The two tendencies converge in the figure of Dr Ibrahim and those of his top lieutenants who belong to the Kobe branch of the Zaghawa. Unlike the Zaghawa Tuer, whose concentration in Sudan provides a large recruiting ground for the SLA, most Kobe live in Chad. Only a minority live in Darfur, concentrated in the Tine area. Many Zaghawa Kobe who do not share Dr Ibrahim's political roots acknowledge that they joined JEM because friends and family already had. If the Kobe connection was ever diminished, or overshadowed by the Islamist connection, they might look elsewhere.

But JEM's leaders insist that their NIF past is just that: past. 'We regional people, especially Darfur, have been very disappointed by the NIF', says Dr Ibrahim, a physician who held a number of regional portfolios before withdrawing from government service in August 1998 and forming an NGO called Fighting Poverty. 'The AIDS of the National Islamic Front is racism.'

Abdullahi el Tom, an academic anthropologist and advisor to the JEM chairman, is a former member of the Communist Party of Sudan. When the two first met in a Paris hotel, over a beer and a glass of orange juice, el Tom asked Dr Ibrahim about Turabi. Ibrahim's response was: 'Everyone of our age has some sort of past. I was part of Turabi but am not at the moment.' El Tom joined JEM in preference to the SLA, which he felt had no coherent philosophy and an absence of institutions.[30] In January 2005, JEM became the first rebel movement to codify its structure, creating a 21-member executive board encompassing all Sudan's regions, a 51-member legislative committee, and a General Congress headed not by a Darfurian, but by an easterner from Blue Nile. Members of the General Congress voted to limit the chairman's term to four years, renewable once. Indicating how far JEM has come from its original, overwhelmingly Islamist roots, they also voted to change the customary Sudanese oath requiring them to obey 'conscience and religion' to 'conscience and cause'.

Support for the NIF in Darfur always had at least as much to do with last-chance politics as with any visceral attachment to radical Islam. In democratic elections in 1986, Darfur voted not for the NIF, but for the Umma party of Sadiq al Mahdi. The Umma failed to deliver for Darfur and Sadiq was discredited by his tolerance of Libyan meddling. The NIF was implicated in the Libyan designs too, but after the 1989 coup Turabi also courted non-Arab groups and developed a genuine constituency in the region. Ten years later, when the ruling party fragmented, Bashir and Ali Osman turned to their own kin – security officers and veteran Islamists, all from the riverine tribes – to fill the most powerful posts in government. Darfurian Islamists rapidly began to desert the ruling Congress Party – less from solidarity with Turabi than from opposition to Bashir and Ali Osman. Dr Ibrahim was outside Sudan at the time, studying for a master's degree in public health at Maastricht University, and denies taking Turabi's side. In 2005, he told UN investigators that Turabi was 'the main reason for the atrocities committed in Darfur'.[31]

Like many of JEM's leaders, Dr Ibrahim was an enthusiastic supporter of the NIF when it seized power in 1989. But by 1993, he says, he was disaffected with the Islamists.

The NIF not only totally neglected our people – it punished our people. It withdrew all services, especially health and education, and by 1994 had stopped paying even a single piastre to the regions. Many schools closed, the number of children in school decreased, and there was a resurgence of illiteracy. In 1991–94, as a regional minister in al Fasher, I got an insight into the government's links to the militias. By 1991, 647 Fur villages had been burned to ashes. Our people started to blame us.

Although he served the NIF for the better part of a decade, and in 1992 spent four months as a volunteer doctor in the paramilitary Popular Defence Forces, Dr Ibrahim never held national office. 'Khalil was not a first or even second class political leader', says his colleague Ahmad Tugod, one of several senior members of JEM who swore an oath, on the Quran, not to support any other political movement – including 'the Islamic movement'.[32] 'He struggled all his life to get a post in Khartoum.' Even before leaving the NIF, several months before the expiry of his term as adviser to the governor of Southern Sudan in Juba, Dr Khalil claims he was taking a different path from most of his colleagues. In al Fasher in 1994, he says, he refused to accept the electricity supply given to ministers and became 'the only minister living in darkness with his people'. As minister for social affairs in Blue Nile in 1997, he fired the northerners who had 'colonized' his department and replaced them with local people. He also dismissed the director of the office for *zakat*, a cousin of President Bashir who was sending all the monies levied by the Islamic tax back to Khartoum. In Juba in 1998, he taxed security officials who had established a monopoly on food shipped into the besieged city and were selling it at a 400 per cent profit. 'In one day', he says, 'I raised 64 million pounds! These security people had never been treated like this…'

From the beginning of the rebellion in Darfur, JEM and the SLA entered into a close military and political alliance. But because many of its leaders have served in government, JEM has political skills, and experience, that the SLA, on the whole, does not have. Its agenda is more clearly focused on the whole Sudanese nation. JEM rejects the Naivasha peace deal, which it considers perpetuates the neglect of the northern peripheries – not just Darfur, but also Kordofan and the Beja Hills of eastern Sudan. Its leaders say the NIF is incapable of reform and admit that JEM cadres in Khartoum were responsible for an attempted coup in September 2004. The government claimed the coup was designed to scuttle Naivasha and spring Turabi from jail. Not so, says Dr Ibrahim. 'Why should we do anything for Hassan Turabi?'

From *The Black Book* to Guerrilla Operations

The roots of JEM go back to 1993, when seven members of the NIF, including Dr Ibrahim, formed a secret cell in al Fasher to discuss reforming the NIF from within. A second cell was formed in Kordofan in 1994, and a third in 1997 in Khartoum. Most of the Khartoum cell were university graduates; many, but not all, were Islamists. One of the group was Abubaker Hamid Nur, today general coordinator of JEM.

'From earliest youth we felt there was a problem, but we but didn't know what it was', says Nur.

There was too much suffering. I travelled 60 kilometres to go to primary school, in Kornoi, when I was 7; 350 kilometres to go to intermediate school, in Geneina; 400 kilometres to go to secondary school, in Fasher; and 1,000 kilometres to go to university, in Khartoum. It was forbidden to speak the Zaghawa language in school. In primary school, the teacher gave us a blue ticket to pass to any boy who spoke Zaghawa. At the end of the day, anyone who had had the ticket was whipped. The whole of Kutum province, with a population of more than 551,000, had one general doctor and no specialists. Women walked more than eight hours daily to get less than 60 litres of water. We were excluded from all key posts and had no way of communicating with the international community to ask for help. Why? Because a gang in Khartoum was controlling everything.[33]

The dissidents decided the first requirement was to educate ordinary Sudanese about the imbalances in Sudan and in 1997 formed a 25-man committee to start collecting information. The result, in May 2000, was *The Black Book*, a political and economic anatomy of marginalization in Sudan. By the time *The Black Book* was published, however, its authors had come to the conclusion that reform from within was impossible and plans were being laid for an armed movement to be called the Justice and Equality Movement. In 2001, they decided to send more than twenty of their leaders outside Sudan in order to bring the opposition 'into the light'. One of them was Khalil Ibrahim. In August 2001, in a press release issued in the Netherlands, he announced the existence of JEM as a political movement. Exactly a year later, Part Two of the *Black Book* appeared on JEM's website. Making clear that JEM was not only fighting against marginalization but also had a national agenda for political change, it called for a 'comprehensive congress' to redress injustices perpetrated by 'a small group of autocratic rulers'.

Even more than the SLA, JEM believes that the problems of Darfur require national solutions. A five-point manifesto made public early in 2003 called for a unified Sudan; justice and equality in place of social injustice and political tyranny; 'radical and comprehensive constitutional reform' that would 'guarantee the regions their rights in ruling the country'; basic services for every Sudanese; and balanced economic and human development in all regions of the country. JEM wants a presidency that rotates among all Sudan's main regions. It rejects the idea that religion is a root cause of Sudan's problem but, unlike the SLA, does not talk about separation of state and religion. It says Islamic law should not be imposed on non-Muslims, 'and the believers of the other faiths must not oppose Muslims' attempts to apply the laws of their religion for themselves'.[34] This wording treads a fine line between constitutional secularism and enshrining Sharia for Muslims. It is a subtle position – perhaps inconsistent, but entirely within the mainstream of northern Sudanese political thought. Sadiq al Mahdi attempts precisely the same balancing act when he insists that rights should be based on citizenship alone, not religious faith, but also argues that Muslims have the right to live in a society governed by Islamic principles.

Although dominated by Zaghawa Kobe, JEM reached out to other tribes – in all marginalized areas – and gave many leadership positions. Nur al Din Dafa'alla, a Missiriya, became Dr Ibrahim's deputy; Khattab Ibrahim Widaa, a Ta'aisha, became deputy spokesman. One of the first to be contacted, in October 2001, was Turabi's second-in-command, Ali al Haj, a Darfurian with a national profile. Al Haj rejected the overture, but in April 2003 joined Dr Ibrahim in the 'Union of the Marginalized Majority', a nationwide coalition which, like JEM itself, united Islamists and anti-Islamists before disappearing off the political map.

While successful in building a broad tribal base, JEM suffered from attempts to divide and rule – both by the Sudan government and, according to Dr Ibrahim, by President Deby. In 2004, JEM's chief of staff, Jibril Abdel Karim, broke away to form the National Movement for Reform and Development, criticizing Dr Ibrahim for running the movement from Europe. The JEM chairman dismissed the criticism: unlike the SLA, he said, JEM's political leadership had always been outside Darfur. He blamed the split on Sudan government efforts to weaken JEM. The claim was credible. Hassan Burgo, a close associate of Salah Gosh and assistant for African affairs in the ruling party, was in contact with Abdel Karim's supporters in Paris before the split. Speaking on al-Jazeera television after the split, Burgo said the NMRD represented the 'real' people of Darfur and sounded the death knoll of JEM. In stark contrast to the slow pace of the mainstream peace talks in Abuja, it took just one day for the NMRD somehow to reach agreement with the NIF.

In 2005, three JEM officers made a second breakaway attempt in collusion with a JEM dissident in N'Djamena, Mohamed Saleh, who had been dismissed from the movement by JEM's executive board and legislative council meeting in joint session. JEM blamed the trouble on President Deby, and alleged he was in the pay of Khartoum. Chadian authorities reacted by cracking down on JEM and arresting eighteen of its members. Dr Ibrahim's verdict was: 'I am not worried about Mohamed Saleh. I am worried about Idriss Deby. There will be more Mohamed Salehs.'

The intellectual roots of JEM lie mainly among disillusioned Islamists, whose frankness and hospitality have attracted others, including secularists for whom the SLA would provide a more natural home if only it were more politically sophisticated. JEM's military capacity, such as it is, lies in its local base among the Zaghawa Kobe. Its main strength is, as it was at the beginning, its organization and its leaders' political experience.

Darfur's rebels are an awkward coalition of Fur and Masalit villagers, Zaghawa Bedouins out of patience with Khartoum, a handful of professionals who dared to take on leadership, and disillusioned Islamist intellectuals. Unlike the first generation of SPLA fighters, who emerged from an army mutiny, few of Darfur's guerrillas had military experience or discipline before they took up arms. The two main rebel groups are united by deep resentment at the marginalization of Darfur, but are not natural bedfellows and could easily be split apart. Theirs is not an insurgency born of revolutionary ideals, but rather a last-ditch response to the escalating violence of the *Janjawiid* and its patrons in Khartoum. In the first months of 2003, these half-formed and inexperienced rebel fronts were catapulted out of obscurity to face challenges for which they were totally unprepared. They should perhaps have had more foresight. Darfur was on the brink of becoming 'southern Sudan speeded up',[35] and several leading members of JEM, if not the SLA, had first-hand experience of that war.

5

The War

As rebellion welled in Darfur throughout 2002, Khartoum's Darfur policy was half-hearted and incoherent, pulled in one direction by the security clique and in another by more thoughtful military and government officials. Sudan's shrewdest politician, Ali Osman Taha, struggled to hold the ring, but his attention was elsewhere – on the South and the improving but rocky relations with America. And at the critical moment, the vice president made his choice: let the war proceed.

Prominent among the officials advocating negotiation was the governor of North Darfur, General Ibrahim Suleiman. A former army chief of staff, and a Berti, General Suleiman tried to address the rebels' grievances through tribal councils and quiet contacts with the rebel leadership. He believed the rebels' demands were negotiable. The SLA were not separatists; they wanted amnesty and recognition as a political movement, a pledge to implement development projects in Darfur and autonomous powers within a federal system – something the government itself mooted eighteen months later, in its first political proposal to end the war. Hilal was something different: General Suleiman considered him a born criminal. Upon taking office in February 2001, the general

had summoned the militia leader and warned him: 'If I decide
to kill you, I will kill you, and nothing will happen to me.'
Hilal just smiled. Suleiman concluded that he knew, even then,
that he couldn't be touched.[1] In August 2002, General Suleiman
arrested Musa Hilal and 23 other 'troublemakers' and sent them
to prison a thousand miles away – in Port Sudan – 'to get them
out of Darfur, to let things quieten down'. Four months later,
Hilal was moved to house arrest in Khartoum, reportedly after
the personal intervention of Ali Osman.

Military Intelligence wanted a show of force. It could overrule
General Suleiman and bully the vice-president. Visiting al Fasher
in November 2002, Ali Osman made clear that a military solution
was on the cards and would be ruthless. He warned that Darfur
would be 'pulled backward for many years' if the rebels followed
the example of the SPLA. There would be total destruction.

The fighting escalated. The rebels announced themselves publicly in February. On 18 March, a fragile ceasefire negotiated by
General Suleiman collapsed after Arab militias ambushed the
most senior Masalit sheikh, 70-year-old Saleh Dakoro, on the
road from Geneina to Kokota village. No one doubted that the
attack was targeted: Sheikh Dakoro was a legendary horseman
and the horse he was riding was known to everyone in Dar
Masalit – including Military Intelligence. The old sheikh survived
the attack, but was wounded and taken to hospital in Khartoum,
where he died within hours of telephoning relatives to say he
would be returning to Darfur 'in a few days'.[2] The word spread
like wildfire: the grand old man of the Masalit, wounded by
the militias in Darfur, had been murdered by the government
in Khartoum! Masalit leaders issued a statement deploring his
death as 'the continuation of a policy of eliminating leaders of
groups and communities accused or suspected of opposing the
government.'[3] They accused the government of 'exploiting the
international focus on the current conflict in Iraq to escalate
human rights abuses in Western Sudan'.

On 25 March, the rebels upped the ante, seizing the garrison town of Tine on the Chad border and capturing huge stocks of arms and equipment. A major counteroffensive was inevitable. 'Khartoum will not negotiate with those who took up arms in Darfur and denied the authority of the state and the law', President Omar al Bashir said in April, addressing an open-air rally in al Fasher. The army would be 'unleashed' to 'crush' the rebellion.

The truth of the matter, well known to Bashir, was that the armed forces had already been 'unleashed' – but to very little avail. They were making no headway against the rebels, whose hit-and-run tactics, using Toyota Land Cruisers crossing the semi-desert at high speed, were proving devastatingly effective. Untrained in desert warfare, the Sudanese army was losing almost every encounter, and the government was relying more and more on its air force. Badly hurt by aerial bombardment of their Jebel Marra stronghold, the rebels were planning an attack that would change the face of the war. Unable to take on the government in the air, they had decided to destroy its planes on the ground.

'The planes are ashes'

Early on the morning of 25 April 2003 – a day behind schedule after Abdalla Abakir's men lost their way in the desert – a joint SLA–JEM force raced across the sand in thirty-three Land Cruisers, entered al Fasher at 5.30 a.m. and attacked the air base as the garrison slept. By the time the operation was over, seven hours later, four Antonov bombers and helicopter gunships were destroyed, by government count, and seven by the rebels'. At least 75 troops, pilots and technicians had been killed and another 32 captured, including the commander of the air base, Maj. Gen. Ibrahim Bushra Ismail. The rebels lost only nine men. Shortly before 9.00 a.m., anxious soldiers waiting for air support in the

Helicopter gunships at Geneina airport, 2004

Kutum area radioed: 'Where are the planes?' The response came back: 'The planes are ashes.'[4]

In more than twenty years' war in the South, the SPLA had never inflicted such a loss on the air force. The rebels were jubilant. 'We went in with twelve Land Cruisers and came out with twenty-one!' one unit commander said: 'The attack changed everything. We got ammunition, vehicles and weapons. Young men flocked to join us.'

This was the pivotal moment of the war. The SLA and JEM, with their lightning attacks, were running rings around the army. Now the armed forces had been publicly humiliated in an unprecedented way. The rebels' military capacity bewildered the government. The Sudanese army would need to be redeployed and retrained to fight this new front with its unfamiliar style of combat, and the large number of Darfurian NCOs and men in the army were conspicuously unwilling to put up much resistance. Although Khartoum insisted publicly that the trouble in Darfur was the work of 'outlaws', some saw in it the hand of the SPLA; others, of Hassan al Turabi, who they suspected was planning an armed takeover of power. The security cabal in Khartoum was fired by rage: its instinctive response was to crush the rebels who had done this, along with anyone who sympathized with them. Military Intelligence took the Darfur file.

The government did initially continue negotiations with the rebels, but only for as long as it took the elders of General Ismail's Misiriya tribe to mediate and obtain his release. Khartoum refused to extend political recognition to the SPLA and instead focused on gearing up its mobilization in a quest for a military solution. A military operational area was declared along the Chad border and a state-wide curfew imposed. More than 150 people were arrested in a security clampdown. For a while, despite the crackdown, the rebel armies kept the upper hand. The SLA destroyed a Sudanese battalion north of Kutum in May, killing 500 soldiers and taking 300 prisoners.[5] Rapidly expanding their area of operations, SLA mobile units launched a surprise attack on Mellit, a big market town north-east of al Fasher. General Suleiman was sacked, made a scapegoat for the al Fasher fiasco.[6] In mid-July, Tine was attacked for the second time and 250 soldiers were killed. SLA forces began infiltrating south and east of Jebel Marra, reaching as far as Um Kedada, towards Kordofan, and Buram, well south of Nyala. The rebels were winning almost every encounter – 34 out of 38 in the middle months of 2003. The government feared it would lose the whole of Darfur, and probably Kordofan too, if their advances continued.

Unleashing the Janjawiid

The government war effort had three main elements: Janjawiid, air force and Military Intelligence. General Suleiman advised against using the Janjawiid, convinced that a racially based mobilization would have 'terrible' repercussions on inter-tribal relations for the next several decades. His solution would have been political and developmental: 'International intervention to eradicate the illiteracy of six million people... Hundreds of schools... Settle the nomads (and give them) water... Well-equipped, well-trained police... Health projects.' But his advice was ignored. Month by month Khartoum ratcheted up its military infrastructure in Darfur – and central to its counterattack was its tried and tested militia strategy. In the subsequent debate over whether the war in Darfur constituted genocide or not – a debate whose burden of proof, paradoxically, became a hindrance to action – one thing is certain: the people who decided to use the Janjawiid as a counterinsurgency force knew exactly what it would mean. They had used similar militias in the Nuba mountains in the early 1990s, and in the contested oilfields of Southern Sudan starting in 1998, and had seen the results. Now they were planning a replay.

In June, Musa Hilal flew back to Darfur. There were recruitment drives all over the region – both for the PDF and for the Janjawiid, and always on a tribal basis. Arab and Masalit omdas were asked to raise volunteers in West Darfur, and in June despatched 6,000 men to army headquarters in Geneina. One of the Masalit omdas, Gamr Musa of Millebeeda, raised 1,000 men. Every single one was rejected. 'The government gave weapons to the Arab youths and sent the Masalit away. They only wanted to see how many Masalit youths there were.'[7] Two hardliners in the security clique – Abdalla Safi al Nur and State Minister for Justice Ali Karti, a former coordinator of the PDF – recruited for the PDF. Karti reportedly 'flew all over Darfur' in an attempt to buy the support of Arab tribal leaders with 50-kilogram sugar sacks full of cash drawn from the coffers of security chief Salah Gosh.[8] Development projects were dangled in front of Arab communities. On 22 November 2003, the governor of South Darfur state, Maj. Gen. Hamid Musa, ordered the recruitment of '300 fursan for Khartoum' in the same breath as he promised to vaccinate camels and horses, and build classrooms, a health unit and 24 water pumps in eight villages.[9]

The Janjawiid were upgraded to a full paramilitary fighting force, with communications equipment as well as plentiful new arms, some artillery, and military advisors. Lending credence to US claims that Musa Hilal returned to Darfur as government-appointed coordinator of Janjawiid activities, Hilal moved thousands of Janjawiid from South Darfur to North Darfur, the launch pad for all major SLA attacks at the time, and organized at a new base for them in Jebel Sirro, west of Kutum.[10]

Hilal's Misteriha barracks now had two main divisions – 'The Light, Swift, and Fearsome Forces' and a smaller rapid-deployment force called the 'Quick Launch Attack'. Across Darfur, there were at least six Janjawiid brigades working alongside the regular armed forces – among them, the *Liwa al Nasr*, or Victory Brigade, of Abdel Rahim Ahmad Mohamed, nicknamed 'Shukurtalla', and the *Liwa al Jammous*, or Buffalo Brigade, of Hamid Dawai. Shukurtalla, an army officer from Wad Medani in central Sudan, had been sentenced to ten years' imprisonment in 2002 for abandoning the southern front. He was released after twelve months and mandated to organize Janjawiid forces in West Darfur, where he terrorized Masalit with the boast that 'I am the Izrael [the angel of death] of the Masalit!' Dawai had also been in jail, accused of killing ten non-Arabs in Beida market in March 1999. A Masalit lawyer who interrogated him in jail, Khamis Yousif Haroun, believed there was enough evidence to convict him. But the Masalit sultan was nervous about moving against such a powerful Arab, and recommended negotiations followed by compensation. Local officials received death threats, and did nothing. Dawai walked free.[11]

Darfur's new army may have closed its doors to the 'African' tribes who were traditionally its mainstay. But in everything else it was undiscriminating, accepting – even seeking out – the

criminal element that was a defining feature of the pre-war
Janjawiid. Musa Hilal set the example. Shortly after returning to
North Darfur, he visited Kutum jail, and ordered the staff to
bring all prisoners before him. One of the warders remembers
him saying, 'Why are Arabs in prison?' and ordering that they
be released. Many such men found a safe haven in the Janjawiid,
whose own behaviour was defined by its unbound criminality.
The Janjawiid stole, burned, mutilated, killed and raped – subjecting
tiny communities to unimaginable horrors. In the village of Har
Jang in North Darfur in April 2004, Janjawiid summarily executed
a group of young men with bullets in the back of the head.
One young man who was the only survivor in his family, having
saved his life by hiding under a dead mule, recounted how the
attackers 'took a knife and cut my mother's throat and threw her
into the well. Then they took my oldest sister and began to rape
her, one by one. My father was kneeling, crying and begging
them for mercy. After that they killed my brother and finally my
father. They threw all the bodies in the well.'[12]

Under Military Intelligence coordination, the official PDF and
the unofficial Janjawiid became indistinguishable. The army supplied
the now paramilitary Janjawiid, accompanied them as they fanned
out to set up bases in outlying villages, surrounded villages as
Janjawiid attacked them, and participated in mopping-up operations
afterwards. By August 2004, four months after Khartoum signed
an agreement to disarm all militias, the Janjawiid were operating
sixteen camps in just one of Darfur's three states.[13] Five of these
camps were shared with regular government forces. Three had
pads for helicopters.

As arms for the expanding Janjawiid brigades rolled in during
October 2003, SLA commanders say the pattern of attacks in Darfur
shifted – from rebel positions in the mountains and foothills to
villages far from the rebels. Fighting between the government
and the rebel groups declined, but Janjawiid attacks on civilians
increased, closely coordinated with air force bombardments. From

the initial rebel strongholds in the north and west of Darfur, the government campaign extended inexorably south and east.

In this way Khartoum fought its war, turning the tide against the rebels. The army usually played a supporting role, as in Urum, near Habila in Dar Masalit, in November 2003.[14]

> The Janjawiid came without the army and burnt 50 per cent of the town. They took the cattle and killed forty-two men, most of them young men. There was a funeral that day for an 80-year-old man, Yahya Abdul Karim, and people were in the mosque reading prayers for him. Sixteen people were killed in the mosque. The imam, Yahya Warshal, ran from the mosque to his home to get his 3-year-old grandson, who was an orphan. The Janjawiid followed him. They killed him and the child. They burned 80 out of 300 huts and stole more than 3,000 cows. Also goats, sheep, horses and donkeys. They wore khaki – the same as the army. Our young men didn't fight. They were running to save themselves. A few weeks later, on 6 or 7 December, the Janjawiid came back at 6 a.m., with the army. The soldiers were in Land Cruisers with doshkas mounted on them. They had one lorry too. The Janjawiid came on horses and camels. The soldiers stayed on the edge of the village while the Janjawiid killed eighty people including women and children. They saw everything...[15]

Less often the army led the way, usually with air support. This was the case in Abun on 13 February 2004.[16]

> At 11.30 a.m. the Janjaweed came on horses and camels and the army in Land Cruisers. The soldiers were the first to come into the village. They killed two men – Ibrahim Ahmad Bakhit, 35, and Ibrahim Idriss Abakir, 40. The two had grabbed their money and were trying to ride away. As they were leaving, the soldiers shot them. Ten minutes later, the Janjawiid came. They searched the village, took clothes and money, and then burned everything including all the food. They tore up Qurans.

Army officers, air force pilots and militia commanders operated in an ethics-free zone, as they had in earlier wars. A government

official who fled to Switzerland, traumatized by what he had
witnessed in the Nuba mountains, said the orders given to the
government forces there had been 'to kill anything that is alive.
That is to say: to kill anybody, to destroy the area, to implement
a scorched earth policy ... so that nothing can exist there.'[17] In
the oilfields, the orders were identical: 'If you see a village, you
burn that village. If you find a civilian, you kill that civilian. If
you find a cow, that cow is your cow!'[18] With the same men in
power in Khartoum, the orders issued in Darfur could only be
the same. As a communiqué to the commander of the 'Western
military area' from Musa Hilal's headquarters in Misteriha said,
citing orders from the president of the Republic: 'You are informed
that directives have been issued... to change the demography of
Darfur and empty it of African tribes' through burning, looting
and killing 'of intellectuals and youths who may join the rebels
in fighting'.[19]

Impunity was an integral, official part of the new order. A
directive issued in North Darfur in February 2004 directed all
security units to 'allow the activities of the Mujahidiin and the
volunteers under the command of Sheikh Musa Hilal to proceed
in the areas of [North Darfur] and to secure their vital needs.'
The directive stressed the 'importance of non-interference', of
not challenging Hilal's men, and instructed local authorities to
'overlook minor offences by the Mujahidiin against civilians who
are suspected members of the rebellion.'[20]

Bombing Darfur

The air force continued in its leading role. Large numbers of
displaced had congregated in Habila by August 2003. It seems
that their presence was the reason why the town was heavily
bombed, killing thirty people on a single day that month. The
UN Commission of Inquiry found 'no evidence that there was any

rebel activity or structures in the vicinity that could have been the target of this attack' and appeared to accept the government explanation that it had been a 'mistake'. Local people disagreed. 'Before the bombing, Tunfunka, Tulus, Andanga, Hajjar and Bayda had all been burned and everyone had run to Habila', said a young man who lost four relatives in Habila. 'The government bombed Habila because it was full of displaced people.'[21]

The government denied that its planes were targeting civilians, but it lied. In January 2004, villagers fleeing a Janjawiid attack in the Um Berro area intercepted, on FM, a radio conversation between an Antonov pilot and an officer called Morad, known to them as army intelligence. 'Morad, Morad', the pilot said. 'Burn everything! Destroy everything!'[22] The following month, a British journalist taped the following radio conversation between an army commander and an Antonov pilot:[23]

Commander: We've found people still in the village.
Pilot: Are they with us or against us?
Commander: They say they will work with us.
Pilot: They're liars. Don't trust them. Get rid of them.
[later] Pilot: Now the village is empty and secure for you. Any village you pass through you must burn. That way, when the villagers come back they'll have a surprise waiting for them.

Raids like these, which needed authorization from the chief of staff's office in Khartoum, made nonsense of the government's insistence that it was not supporting Janjawiid operations. As one of the displaced said: 'We know the Arabs. They don't have planes; they have cows! Only the government has planes!'[24] The raids continued even after the government agreed to halt military flights. On the very day that Khartoum agreed to halt its flights, in December 2004, seven government aircraft were simultaneously bombarding the Labado area east of Nyala.

With air support, the Janjawiid spread out across Darfur, attacking defenceless communities. Villagers were killed in their hundreds

– shot, stabbed, burned alive, and butchered.[25] Bodies were mutilated and left in the open, there to be seen by anyone who might consider returning. In one village, sixty-six villagers were tortured in the local dispensary before being killed – some hanged by their feet, others decapitated.[26] In another, schoolgirls were chained together and burned alive.[27] 'You believe there's an inherent goodness in people, but you see some of these villages and it shakes that belief', said Colonel Barry Steyn, commander of the AU's small South African contingent. 'You look at this stuff and it makes you turn white.'[28]

The Janjawiid rarely attacked the guerrillas in their mountain bases. The few policemen who had patrolled Darfur had long since withdrawn. This left villages like Urum and Abun as easy pickings. A confidential UN report compiled in March 2004 said the 'total disengagement' of services and supplies in Darfur allowed the government to justify its attacks by claiming the villages into which it sent its forces were under rebel control.

> Supplies and salaries are not paid any longer, leaving communi-
> ties in a vacuum where law and order are precarious.... These
> villages are then alleged to have passed under SLA control....
> Based on the assumption that the SLA is present in the village,
> the eviction process starts.... If people do not move immediate-
> ly, a second more deadly attack is launched and civilians are left
> with no option but to move away to the nearest 'safe haven',
> which is usually also attacked within the next few days.... Even
> when the village has been emptied of its inhabitants, Janjawiid
> may go back and totally destroy what is left.[29]

The Janjawiid not only murdered. They also targeted women with sexual violence – a feature of the war in the Nuba mountains, but seldom before seen in Darfur. Rape was so ubiquitous that it appeared to be an instrument of policy to destroy the fabric of the targeted communities and perhaps even to create a new generation with 'Arab' paternity. 'These rapes are... orchestrated to create a dynamic where the African tribal groups are destroyed', an aid worker said. 'It's hard to believe that they tell them they want to make Arab babies, but it's true. It's systematic.'[30] Nor was sexual violence limited to rape. Early in 2003, a young woman called Mariam Ahmad was stopped at a roadblock and forced to watch while Janjawiid cut the penis off her 21-day-old son, Ahmad.[31] The child died soon after in her arms. In Bargai, a village near Zalingei, a young mother who had just given birth to twins was killed with her legs tied to her neck, exposing her genitals. Her babies were thrown into a container of boiling water that had been brought for the birth.[32]

Despite government claims that the rebels were merely brigands and criminals, the vast majority were farmers whose homes had been destroyed and who faced unenviable choices: to live as refugees in Chad, suffer displacement and continued persecution in Darfur, or separate from their families and take up arms. There is strong evidence, as yet insufficiently examined, that the government, on more than one occasion, went gunning for the displaced precisely because it knew that displaced men were flocking to join the rebel movements.

The third prong of the deadly triad was Military Intelligence itself, the architect, arbiter and, often, executioner of the Darfur campaign. In December 2003, Security and Janjawiid worked hand-in-glove to destroy a swathe of Wadi Saleh which was full of displaced Fur and Masalit. Thirty-two villages and hamlets along Wadi Debarei were burned – among them Bindisi, Arwala, Sindu and Nankose – and displaced villagers packed into the once-prosperous market town of Deleig. Over a period of weeks 172 people were captured and killed in Deleig. Many had their throats cut and their bodies thrown in the stagnant pools of a seasonal river just south of the town.[33] The burning continued. On 5 March 2004, the frightened community around Wadi Debarei woke up to find a wide area surrounded by soldiers and Janjawiid who began going from shelter to shelter and hut to hut, asking each man for his home village. Armed with a list of 200 names of 'SLA

Shoba village, near Kebkabiya, burned by the Janjawiid, 2002

leaders' drawn up by a local intelligence chief, Ibrahim Jumaa, security officers took away more than 100 men – almost all of them displaced. In the evening, 71 of them – the 'SLA leaders' – were put in army trucks and taken from the police station to a wadi, where they were lined up, forced to kneel and shot in the back of the head.[34] A similar massacre took place in the Mukjar area further south. In all, at least 145 men were executed in Deleig and Mukjar that night. Another 58 were killed in the Deleig area the following day.[35]

Security's counterinsurgency converged with the local Janjawiid agenda of land and chieftaincies. A week before the massacre, nine Fur *omdas* had been arrested. All nine were shot dead in prisons in Mukjar and Garsila, near Deleig, on the same night as the mass executions in the wadis – clearing the way for the Salamat and Mahariya to take possession of the area.

Despite government commitments to do both, Janjawiid were neither disarmed nor arrested. Instead the government opted for denial and, when that failed, deception. Common crimi-

Mass funeral of victims of the Janjawiid, Shoba, 2002

nals arrested before the rebellion were paraded as Janjawiid and then executed. Sham disarmament ceremonies were organized for visitors. On 27 August 2004, the UN Special Representative witnessed 300 Janjawiid in Geneina hand over their weapons. Locals said they were handed back the following day.[36] In January 2005, the UN's Independent Commission of Inquiry reported that the government had been able to cite only one case of punishment since the rebellion began – that of a man who, apparently acting on his own initiative, had burned a single village, Halouf, with the loss of twenty-four lives.[37]

Creating Famine

Government and Janjawiid forces destroyed everything that made life possible. Food that could be carried away was; the rest was burned. Animals that could be taken away were; the rest were killed. The simple straw buildings that served as clinics and schools were destroyed, usually simply with matches, and everything in them was stolen or torched. Pumps were smashed and wells polluted – often with corpses. Mosques were burned and Qurans desecrated. In the first year of the rebellion, more than sixty-two mosques were burned in West Darfur alone.[38] It was, the UN Commission of Inquiry said, 'a nightmare of violence and abuse' that stripped villagers of the very little they had. Worse: except in a few cases, the abuses had reportedly occurred 'without any military justification'. The UN estimated that between 700 and 2,000 villages were totally or partially destroyed.

By the beginning of 2005, almost 2 million people had been driven to overcrowded and unsanitary camps inside Darfur[39] and another 200,000 had sought refuge in Chad. Humanitarian catastrophe was a deliberate act. These destitute and displaced people were deterred from searching for wild foods or from gathering firewood by the threat of rape or death at the hands of Janjawiid bands. The government also deployed long years of expertise in delaying and blocking relief operations with a farrago of bureaucratic entanglements. Aid workers needed visas to enter Sudan, travel permits to Darfur, daily travel permits to leave the state capitals,[40] and fuel permits to travel around Darfur. UNICEF drugs needed to save lives were taken for testing in Sudanese labs. Vehicles were held up in Port Sudan, and on reaching Darfur were frequently impounded. In mid-2004, as rains threatened epidemics in overcrowded displaced camps, rigorous registration requirements for health workers impeded the ability of relief agencies to respond to disease.[41] By year-end, Jan Egeland, head of the UN's Office for the Coordination of Humanitarian Affairs, estimated that 10,000 people were dying every month.[42]

Starvation was not mere negligence. As before in the South and Nuba Mountains, it was military strategy.[43] Left to their own devices, rural people in Darfur can usually find enough sustenance from wild foods to see them through months of hunger.[44] 'We don't just starve: someone must force starvation upon us', an old woman said in 1986, explaining how her family had survived the great famine of 1984–85.[45] Death rates in Darfur tripled in that crisis and some 100,000 people perished – mostly children and old people. That was bad enough, but in 2004 the Janjawiid forcibly obstructed coping strategies, and people died in far larger numbers. A UN team that visited Kailek camp in South Darfur in April 2004 found a death rate 41 times higher than the standard threshold for an 'emergency'. Among under-5s, the death rate was 147 times higher.[46] Accusing government forces of a 'strategy of systematic and deliberate starvation', the UN described how armed men 'guarding' the displaced had stopped food entering the camps – even the wild foods collected by the displaced themselves – and had taken it for themselves and their camels. Had Kailek not been exposed, how many other starvation camps might have been established?

When anger over conditions in the camps became too great to continue to deny access to them, the government simply 'disappeared' them. In July 2004, UN Secretary General Kofi Annan visited one of Darfur's worst camps in a deserted plant nursery in the centre of al Fasher. On arrival, he found stagnant puddles and dead donkeys, but no people. No one believed the assertion that it had been cleared because it had no sanitation.[47] Annan also visited Mashtel camp outside al Fasher and found it, too, empty. Only twenty-four hours previously, aides had seen it 'brimming' with life. A government official said the displaced had been moved to the outskirts of al Fasher because Mashtel would flood when the rains came; he denied the move had been to stop Annan bearing witness. But the manner, and the timing, of the move suggested otherwise: the displaced were simply loaded into army trucks and dumped at the gates of the already overcrowded Abu Shouk camp, where some 40,000 people were living in open desert.

When Khartoum could not stop humanitarian efforts, it sought to co-opt them into its war strategy. In July 2004, President Bashir's special representative in Darfur, Interior Minister General Abdel

Market in Muzbat, Dar Zaghawa, 2005

Rahim Mohamed Hussein, announced a plan to 'settle' more than a million displaced in eighteen locations where they would be given 'services and protection' and 'trained in carrying weapons so they can take part in defending themselves'.[48] The plan was a rerun of the 'peace villages' project in the Nuba mountains, where Nuba burned out of their homes were herded together in brutal, well-guarded concentrations near garrison towns while Arabs took over their land.

While most Darfurians grew ever poorer, Janjawiid commanders and security officers profited from a new war economy of loot and extortion, growing rich on the misery of others – Arab and non-Arab. Janjawiid units and individual militiamen ran mafia-like operations. Janjawiid at road blocks demanded money from passing cars, on pain of death. In 2004, a confidential UN report said residents of Birka Saira, an ethnically mixed town fifty miles west of Misteriha, had had 1.8 million dinars 'extorted' from them in nine months – a huge sum in a poor community where a day's labour, when labour there was, brought only 200 dinars. This was not the work of rogue elements. In May 2004, the Military Intelligence office of Musa Hilal's Misteriha headquarters demanded $4,000 in ransom for *omda* Khidir Ali Rahman of Tur, a Fur village.[49] Hilal had led *Janjawiid* into Tur on 27 March 2004, again wearing his colonel's uniform. As his men went through the village like locusts, stealing even the carpet from the mosque, he sent a military vehicle to bring *omda* Ali Rahman to him. Almost two months later, the *shartai* of the Fur received a ransom note, which concluded: 'For the urgent resolution of this matter, please send the money as soon as possible. If you do not, his fate will be in your hands.'

Keeping the Secret

Crimes like those being committed in Darfur did not bear scrutiny. From the very start of the rebellion, the government did everything in its power to black out all news from, and comment on, the region. The correspondent of the *Al-Sahafa* newspaper in Nyala, Yusuf al Bashir Musa, was arrested after publishing a report on the rebel attack on al Fasher, accused of 'spreading false information against the state', and severely beaten with sticks on his body and the sole of his only foot. Amnesty International suggested that the torture of Musa, who had already had one leg amputated, helped to intimidate other journalists thereafter. 'Red lines' issued to journalists included a prohibition against mentioning human rights abuses in Darfur.[50] Independent newspapers that pushed the bar, like the the Arabic-language *Al-Ayam* and the English-language *Khartoum Monitor*, were suspended. Al-Jazeera, the most-watched television station in the Arab world, was closed after it became the first station in the world to report the atrocities in Darfur. Parliament was not allowed to discuss Darfur.

When the international community finally began to show concern over Darfur, access was simply refused. Journalists and human rights investigators were denied visas. This was nothing new: the government had never shown much inclination to let outsiders travel anywhere in Sudan. But as refugees streamed into Chad, and journalists were able to investigate there what they were unable to investigate in Darfur, measures of a different kind were needed. And so, in March 2004, army lorries rounded up Masalit tribal leaders near the border with Chad and took them to the town of Misterei, then under the control of the *Janjawiid* leader Hamid Dawai. Dawai offered the Masalit 250 million dinars to 'create security in the Masalit area so no one can cross the border to Chad'. The Masalit chiefs replied: 'We don't like your security and we don't want your money.' Dawai replied: 'If you don't make this security, I will kill all your civilians.'[51] In the weeks that followed, his men burned dozens of villages around Misterei, creating a no-man's land along the border.

As Darfur began making headlines and it became impossible to refuse all access, the pressure to keep silent grew. Sudanese human rights activists who met foreigners were arrested and held in preventative detention under emergency legislation that denied them not only access to lawyers, families and medical assistance, but also the right to be brought promptly before a judge, to challenge the legality of their detention and to be treated humanely.[52] International NGOs found themselves facing a bleak choice: to turn a blind eye to atrocities, or to speak out and risk being expelled. In May 2004, two *omdas* were arrested in North Darfur after giving the International Committee of the Red Cross information on burnt villages and mass graves.[53] Another fifty people were arrested between 26 June and 3 August 2004, most of them after speaking to foreign delegations. In South Darfur, police were posted outside Nyala hospital to keep journalists away from villagers wounded in *Janjawiid* attacks.[54] In West Darfur, Masalit community leaders were arrested on suspicion of passing information to foreigners about attempts to force the displaced to return to their homes and, by extension, to starve in burned areas that were not receiving relief.

Secrecy was not only essential to Khartoum's war; it was also key to its local allies' plans for regional supremacy. In November 2003, a confidential report by the political committee of the Arab Gathering on a series of meetings with local leaders in South Darfur sketched out a 'project' for 'the complete domination of power' in Darfur, as an example for 'the whole of Sudan'. This included recruiting and organizing *Janjawiid* and extending (Arab) 'unity deep into the Republic of Chad'.[55] Time and again the report called for caution: 'Secrecy is required for the successful development of the project'... 'Secrecy is important'... 'Importance of secrecy in all internal steps'.[56]

What was Khartoum's calculation? How could it inflict such atrocities on a civilian population, creating such a humanitarian catastrophe, and expect to escape crisis at home and censure abroad? One part of the answer is that the Darfur file was in the hands of Security, which cared not at all about internal dissent or external pressure. Indeed, many security officers were opposed to concessions made in the North–South peace talks in Kenya and would have been quite happy to see those negotiations collapse. With Darfur screened off by the security agencies, the rest of the government went into denial. But it is also true that the government leaders who authorized the campaigns miscalculated. They thought it would be a quick fix, like the suppression of Daud Bolad's incursion in 1991. And because Darfur has neither Christians nor oil, in any significant quantities, they thought that the Western world, happy to see peace in the South at last, would give them a free hand in Darfur. On both fronts, they got it badly wrong.

6

Endgame

Alpha Oumar Konaré feels at home in Darfur. Before being chosen to head the African Union in July 2003, he had been the democratically elected president of Mali, and toured the desert-edge villages and nomadic encampments seeking peace with Tuareg rebels. He is used to arguing with chiefs and guerrillas, and pioneered a campaign, unique in Africa, to eliminate small arms, overseeing 'flame of peace' ceremonies where Kalashnikovs and grenades were burned on gigantic bonfires. Usually dressed in Muslim robes, he could easily be mistaken for a Darfur sheikh. Africa's top civil servant is no well-pressed bureaucrat, cocooned in an air-conditioned Land Cruiser. Visiting Darfur for the first time in June 2004, Konaré gave his entourage the slip and, accompanied by just one security officer, spent the night in a displaced camp. He wanted to see how Darfurians were living, he said. Solving the crisis of Darfur was the African Union's first big test and he was determined to succeed.

The African Union (AU) was established in Durban, South Africa in 2002, taking over from the nearly moribund Organization of African Unity (OAU). Its constitution requires that half of its ten commissioners are women and the top post is that of 'chairperson'.

Chairperson Konaré runs the AU like a chief. He is impatient, domineering and tireless, insistent that lasting peace must come from the grassroots. Darfur was first discussed at the AU's Peace and Security Council in May 2004. In the session, held at AU headquarters in Addis Ababa, Konaré insisted that the Sudanese ambassador make his presentation, but then leave the chamber for the rest of the debate. When the commander of the AU peace-keeping mission in Darfur has been outspoken in criticizing the Khartoum government – by whose consent AU peacekeepers are in Darfur – Konaré has backed him up. 'Africa must not only act in Darfur', he says, 'Africa must be seen to act.'

The African Union became peacemaker in Darfur by default. President Idriss Deby of Chad had begun mediating between the government and rebels in September 2003, but achieved nothing more than a 45-day ceasefire that neither side respected. Peacekeepers were needed, and at the next round of talks in April 2004 the AU was tasked with sending them. The AU advance party arrived within six weeks, a rapid start for an organization that had little experience in peacekeeping. The full AU force was small in number – only 3,000 men for a large and complex region – and severely deficient in transport and communica-tions equipment. It was slow to get on the ground, and took eight months to reach full strength. But its biggest drawback was its mandate. It was tasked only with protecting the small, 120-member ceasefire monitoring group – not the civilians of Darfur who most needed protection. The monitors were out-spoken, even warning, in November 2004, that the government was planning an offensive. But they were novices compared to the Sudan government, which had two decades of experience in impeding humanitarian operations.

On the eve of the April talks in N'Djamena, Deby asked the AU to assist his mediation. As his envoy, Konaré nominated the former prime minister of Niger, Hamid Elgabid, who had served as secretary general of the Organization of the Islamic

Conference. Elgabid found himself in a role for which he was sorely unprepared. Because he did not speak English, French translation slowed down every session. Whenever the delegates got into heated disagreement, he called for adjournment. Successive meetings in N'Djamena and Addis Ababa were disorganized and slow. This played right into the hands of the Khartoum delegation. Headed by Majzoub al Khalifa, the hardline minister of agriculture who has ties to the Arab Gathering, the government negotiators stonewalled, playing for time while the Janjawiid carried on burning and killing. They worked hard to split the SLA from JEM, which they accused of being a front for Turabi. By the time of the Addis Ababa meeting in July, Khartoum's disregard for its solemn commitments was so egregious that even Elgabid's Chadian co-chair – Foreign Minister Mahamat Saleh Annadif, a Rizeigat Arab – openly supported the rebels' complaint that it was pointless to negotiate with an adversary whose promises were not worth the paper they were written on. In Addis Ababa, the rebel leaders were also disappointed: despite having a plane dispatched to pick them up, neither Abdel Wahid al Nur nor Khalil Ibrahim attended. The peace talks promised to be long and frustrating, dogged by incompetence and bad faith on all sides.

In both peacekeeping and peacemaking, the AU had been thrown in at the deep end, and it was floundering. It had fewer staff working on Sudan than the Darfur unit of a medium-sized international NGO. Said Djinnit, the veteran Algerian diplomat who serves as the AU's Commissioner for Peace and Security, found himself drafted in as head of peacekeeping in addition to overseeing the peace negotiations, handling ongoing conflicts in Côte d'Ivoire, Burundi and the Democratic Republic of Congo, and keeping a watchful eye out for new crises. In September, Elgabid was replaced by an experienced AU diplomat, Sam Ibok, and tradecraft improved. Ibok began preparing detailed political framework documents for discussion. But the AU's meagre means were still a far cry from the resources that the troika of the US, Great Britain and Norway had thrown into the marathon North–South negotiations. 'The AU doesn't even have the capacity to start building capacity', complained one experienced military observer.

Things were no better in the rebel camp. The SLA and JEM negotiating teams were catapulted into major negotiations with almost no experience or preparation. Lacking political structures and strategy, the SLA compensated for lack of quality with quantity and sent ever-larger numbers to the talks. Realizing they needed political guidance, they drafted in Sharif Harir of the SFDA. Harir proved the most adept negotiator, but his presence stoked jealousies among younger commanders and by the time of the talks in Abuja the SLA delegation was on the wrong side of forty. Most of its delegates were poorly prepared at best, but still insisted on being party to every discussion. 'It's as though the government had brought the parliament along as well', said one of the mediation team. Abdel Wahid rarely turned up or sent clear instructions. JEM was more disciplined, but Khalil Ibrahim directed his negotiators, as he did his commanders, from afar – by phone from Eritrea or France. The rebels, who hadn't agreed on a political platform, said they would not talk about political substance until Khartoum kept its promises to stop attacking, allow unimpeded humanitarian relief efforts, and disarm the *Janjawiid*. Without a negotiating strategy – and, most importantly, without the leverage of a major power behind them – the talks did not get beyond acrimonious preliminaries. By the end of the year, there had not been a single day's discussion about a framework for a political settlement.

Such disorder is depressingly familiar from wars across Africa, including Southern Sudan and, in earlier years, Chad – where the word 'warlord' first gained currency in the continent. Armed men are given legitimacy as decision-makers for people who have not elected them, and any early idealism is tarnished by the brutal reality of war. In the AU's conference chambers, SLA delegates rage at the government, but don't articulate a political agenda.

Centres fall apart. 'We should be talking about two or three separate
SLAs', says one observer. 'The only thing keeping Abdel Wahid and
Minni talking to each other is that the Americans insist that they
have one delegation.' War economies – smuggled guns, looted
livestock, stolen food aid, taxes – create a criminal momentum
of their own. Governments cannot control the forces they unleash
and make commitments in the full knowledge that they cannot
be implemented. Khartoum knew well that it could not disarm
the Janjawiid even if it wanted to, despite repeated promises to do
just that in 2004. 'We will not retreat', Musa Hilal warned in a
statement sent to 'the leaders of the state' early in 2004 and copied
to 'the loyal, honourable fighters of the masses of our nation'.
The 'cowardly, invalid decision' to disarm the Janjawiid would be
'impossible' to enforce. His men would not surrender their arms.
'God is great. We continue on the road of jihad.' As a former
Islamist who knows the Janjawiid well says, 'The Arab Gathering
existed without government support before today's Janjawiid came
into being. The Janjawiid don't need the government.'

Two years after the rebellion in Darfur became impossible to
ignore, the international community is still in disarray. At least
10,000 lives are being lost each month to disease, hunger and
violence. Warning signs are flashing for another drawn-out cycle
of conflict, political and military fragmentation, recrimination and
famine. Konaré is adamant that Darfur can avoid this fate, and be
the first proof of Africa's resolve and capacity to stop a crime against
humanity. But he will need much more than his overburdened
secretariat, few scattered peacekeepers and solemn words in the
AU's Peace and Security Council to end Darfur's agony.

Forward to the Past

Saeed Mahmoud Ibrahim Musa Madibu ranks alongside the Masalit
sultan as Darfur's most prestigious paramount chief. His official
title is Nazir General, and he heads the Baggara Rizeigat, the

most powerful single tribe in all of Darfur. In his mid-seventies, possessed of a steely presence, he may prove to be Darfur's best hope for peace. He has inherited his ancestors' shrewd calculus of how best to guide his tribe across the shifting sands of the region's politics. He knows the history of both Abbala and Baggara Rizeigat intimately – it was, after all, his grandfather who last held paramount authority over the troublesome northern sections back in 1925. His elder brother Hassan was loyal to Khartoum all his life, and allowed thousands of Rizeigat to fight for the government against the SPLA. But since succeeding Hassan as *nazir* in 1990, Saeed Madibu has tried to steer a course between Khartoum, the SPLA and the Arab Gathering. When he realized the war in the South was unwinnable, he facilitated a local truce with the SPLA. When members of his tribe made inflammatory statements about Arab supremacy, he reprimanded them. (Like all Darfurian Arabs, Madibu has mixed ancestry and is as dark as his 'African' neighbours.) Most importantly, Nazir Madibu refused to throw his tribe behind the *Janjawiid* war, realizing that good neighbourly relations in his own backyard were more important than fighting for a capricious and faraway government.

Yet the old chief never faced a challenge comparable to the war in Darfur, and his nerve and authority were tested to the full as the conflict escalated. Government ministers tried to buy the backing of his tribe, and the governor of South Darfur tried to undermine him by recruiting elements of the Rizeigat militia to the *Janjawiid*. Then, in July 2004, the SLA extended its operations into south-eastern Darfur, looting Rizeigat cattle, attacking villages and threatening to plunge the hitherto calm Rizeigat land into bloody conflict. The Rizeigat militia fought back fiercely, and chased the SLA troops back towards their base at Muhajiriya. Seeking to avoid escalation, Nazir Saeed instructed his men to fall back to their own tribal land and not to storm Muhajiriya. When the SLA persisted, and tried to encircle the Rizeigat, Nazir Saeed sent an ultimatum: desist or we will attack. The SLA desisted.

Without the endorsement of elders of the standing of Nazir Saeed Madibu, Khartoum's Darfur war carries no legitimacy among the majority of Darfur's Arabs – the Baggara tribes that have, in the main, held aloof from the war. Saeed Madibu has not only refused to join the government's campaign. He has also been quietly mobilizing the Native Administration – tribal aristocrats who are conservative but not reactionary, wedded to their own hierarchies and passionate believers in peace and stability. The repository of family genealogies, they know that racial divides are seldom absolute and always less important than good neighbourly relations.

As North and West Darfur burned, the Rizeigat tribal council in al Da'ien protected displaced non-Arabs who had sought refuge in their territory. Nazir Saeed negotiated an agreement with the neighbouring Birgid, a non-Arab tribe, to ensure that any 'misunderstandings' that might arise would not lead to bloodshed, and delegated his tribal council to establish non-aggression pacts with tribes one step further away – Daju, Beigo and Berti. He took special care to work out a reconciliation with the neighbouring Ma'aliya Arabs, a tribe that is junior to the Rizeigat and, resentful of its inferior rank, has clashed violently with them on occasion in the past forty years. In September 2004 the indefatigable *nazir* joined a delegation of twenty-eight tribal elders to Abuja. He was tough with the SLA and JEM leaders – as the government, in allowing him to go, hoped he would be – and insisted that violence would solve nothing. But the government had not anticipated his next step. Growing in confidence, the tribal leaders flew to Tripoli a month later to participate in a promising peace initiative from an unlikely quarter: Colonel Gaddafi. The delegation was headed by General Ibrahim Suleiman, and Khartoum expected nothing more than a talking shop. Unexpectedly, Gaddafi didn't take Khartoum's side but instead encouraged the emergent 'Darfur Tribes Initiative'. The pro-Khartoum and pro-rebel delegations found much to agree upon – most significantly, that they should stick with the old *hakura* system of land possession and that the Native Administration should be independent of government interference.

In Libya, Darfur's tough old chiefs resolved to rebuild a conservative social order on the pillars of peace, stability and tolerance. Their progress in Tripoli emboldened elders all across Darfur to seek their own solutions. In north-east Darfur, an initiative to reconcile the Meidob and Zayadiya has made steady progress. Elders sat to discuss local issues at their own chosen pace, with no artificial pressures. The Meidob and Zayadiya do not covet each other's land and, in the absence of major atrocities, criminal accountability is not an issue for them. In Geneina, Arab and Masalit leaders have hammered out a compromise about tribal hierarchy: the Arabs will keep their *amirs*, but the original system of electing the sultan will remain – ensuring that it stays with the Masalit. Pre-existing land rights will be respected. The chiefs have even done what the government so far has not done: attempt to call Musa Hilal to heel. Anxious to salvage the reputation of their tribe, Rizeigat elders have pressured Hilal to reach out to Fur and Masalit elders. The *Janjawiid* commander has done so – in person in Tripoli, and over the phone. His defence, to all of them, has been that he is only following government orders.

As they struggle to fill Darfur's vacuum of government, the sheikhs are acutely aware of the limits of their power. They know that inter-tribal agreements cannot, on their own, remove the warmongers and war criminals. Thirty conferences over twenty years have not solved Darfur's problems. Today, as before, Khartoum is trying every stratagem to block, bribe, threaten, co-opt or discredit tribal leaders' initiatives. It has stalled the Meidob–Zayadiya reconciliation. When the Libyans issued invitations for a follow-up meeting in January 2005, the government rescinded most of the exit visas it had issued to the tribal delegation and instead nominated a new, hand-picked set of representatives. But no minister was powerful enough to remove Nazir Saeed from the list, even though his opponents in Khartoum were spreading rumours that he had thrown his lot in with the rebels, who already had a Rizeigat in command of their southern front. The old chief went to Libya and stuck to his guns, and Khartoum's loyalists were unable to reverse the progress made in October. But government pressure ensured there were no further compromises with the rebels and their sympathizers on key issues such as Darfur's representation in the central government, amnesty or prosecution for those accused of war crimes, and whether Darfur should stay as three states or be reunited.

Fearing Nazir Saeed Madibu's powers of conciliation, the government reshuffled the Native Administration of South Darfur even as the delegates prepared to leave for Tripoli. In an unprecedented step, Khartoum dismissed *Magdum* Ahmed Rijal of Nyala – the state's most senior Fur chief – and elevated several *omdas* to the status of *nazir*. The government did not dare tamper with the status of Nazir Saeed Madibu himself. But, in a direct challenge to his authority and to the Rizeigat–Ma'aliya agreement he had engineered just three months earlier, it gave Adam Sharif Salim, the chief of the Ma'aliya, equal rank as Nazir. Hitherto loyal Rizeigat in the government began to ask themselves what chaos lay in store for them if Khartoum was playing divide-and-rule with its friends. Visibly tired, Nazir Saeed Madibu will need all his strength and resolve if he is to prevail.

The UN and the Genocide Question

The war in Southern Sudan was fought for twenty-one years, and claimed more than a million lives, without ever reaching the Security Council. Darfur was raised at the Council in May 2004, five months after Mukesh Kapila, the UN's own representative in Khartoum, called it 'the world's greatest humanitarian crisis'. Kapila's contract was not renewed and many in the UN were happy to see him go. They thought him too confrontational.

Darfur was the problem no one wanted to acknowledge. The war hit the headlines just as the Naivasha negotiations were entering their critical phase. The governments that were backing Naivasha – the USA, Britain and Norway – did not want their attention diverted. France was chiefly interested in keeping Chad stable. When the AU took up the file, the Security Council was more than happy to invoke the 'Brahimi principle', named after the Algerian diplomat who in 2000 authored a report proposing that regional organizations take primary responsibility for the problems in their own backyards. Already overburdened with intractable problems, the UN was all too happy to leave Darfur to the AU. But the AU can succeed only if powerful states offer leverage and resources to support it.

The UN and Western governments have had some strong words, but their catalogue of actions to stop the slaughter in Darfur is unimpressive. The only concrete actions in 2003–4 were an arms embargo on Darfur, which, if enforced, would hurt only the rebels, and an international travel ban on named leaders of the Janjawiid (who still managed to fly to Libya unopposed). A proposal to widen the arms embargo to include the Sudanese army would be opposed by Russia, which is selling MiGs to Khartoum. A ban on Sudanese oil exports would be blocked by China, the biggest investor in the Sudanese oilfields. 'Smart' sanctions on leading members of the government – freezing their assets abroad – have been canvassed, but American and British diplomats consider them 'difficult' to implement. The contrast with the absolutism and the determination of the war against terror could not be greater. All these actions, and more, would be automatic if the target were al Qaeda.

In June 2004, the UN Security Council passed Resolution 1556. Its key points were calls for the disarming of the Janjawiid, the arrest of their leaders, and unobstructed humanitarian access, all within thirty days. Forcible disarmament of the Janjawiid is almost certainly impossible – Musa Hilal himself has said as much – even though the Sudan government has committed itself, on more than one occasion, to doing it. Arriving in Sudan a few weeks after the resolution was passed, the new UN Special Envoy, Jan Pronk, a former development minister of the Netherlands, thought it wise to give Khartoum a little more leeway. He believed the UN was setting itself up to fail by asking for the impossible. Instead, he proposed a ninety-day plan with more modest goals – some of which, like 'safe areas' around garrison towns, actually furthered Khartoum's counterinsurgency. At the end of the ninety days, the government had done nothing except partially to ease humanitarian access. A month later, it launched another offensive, cynically depicting it as a 'road-clearing operation'. Under fire from the AU, Khartoum eventually promised to withdraw its troops – but on the very same day ordered them to advance again. It agreed to halt 'offensive' military flights, but soon afterwards bombed the village of Hamada, killing at least sixty-nine civilians.[1] Janjawiid leaders were allowed to roam free. Entire Janjawiid units were 'merged into the police, military and security organs and are now in position', according to Colonel Abdel Wahid Saeed Ali Saeed, the army commander of Misteriha.

Khartoum crossed the Security Council's red line. Nothing happened. Then it crossed Pronk's more generous red line. Still nothing happened. The government's calculation must have been that it could get away with murder. It had an ace in its hand: to make, or break, peace in the South.

All through 2004, Sudanese officials hinted that they would stall the peace process to end Africa's longest war if the world got tough on Darfur. The Naivasha Agreements are a zero-sum deal, dividing power in Sudan between the government and the SPLA. Inviting other opposition groups to the table to claim a share risked putting the negotiations back to square one, if not even derailing them altogether. For a few months in the summer, US and British diplomats considered seeking a quick fix in Darfur before completing the Naivasha process. But when peace talks failed again in Abuja in September, it was clear that there was no quick fix and Naivasha became the priority again. The 'Comprehensive Peace Agreement' was signed in January 2005, and preserving it became the overriding concern. Rebel demands for a share in the interim government, including a vice-presidential post, were ruled out of court because they were not in the CPA.

The Security Council did, however, take a simple step with far-reaching consequences. In passing Resolution 1564 on 18 September 2004, it mandated an International Commission of Inquiry on Darfur (ICID) to investigate human rights violations and ascertain whether genocide had occurred. This was a shot aimed right at the heart of the security cabal in Khartoum. And Bashir had only himself to blame for allowing it to happen.

Alpha Konaré agonized over how to pursue justice without jeopardizing attempts to make peace. In Mali, as in Darfur, the tribal tradition is to conclude a peace agreement by paying *diya* (blood money) and then extending amnesty. Konaré's Malian peace process concluded with a general amnesty voted by parliament, and some tribal leaders in Darfur are advocating something similar today.

Under the Naivasha process, Khartoum and the SPLA, both of which have war criminals in their commands, were allowed to escape with a blanket amnesty for their crimes. Justice was quietly put aside. The warring parties divided up government posts and funds, and pushed democratization down the schedule. Early promises to investigate human rights violations were forgotten in the final 'comprehensive' agreement. There will not even be a truth-and-reconciliation commission. Without impunity, the deal would not have been accepted by the all-powerful men in Khartoum's security cabal.

Like a cancer, these men have taken over the backbone of the state. Their humanity has been withered by sixteen years or more of total power, and human life means nothing to them. When talks began, they were absolutely confident that the AU would be a soft touch. Although founded on constitutional rule, and mandated to intervene to stop gross human rights abuses, the AU had only intervened before in countries with little international clout, like Sierra Leone. But in August 2004, Konaré surprised Bashir by proposing to him the idea of an African inquiry into Darfur similar to the international Panel the OAU set up after the Rwandan genocide. The Panel wrote a fine report with human rights at its centre and recommendations framed by the politics of peace and stability. Konaré's envoy met with Sudanese Foreign Minister Mustafa Osman Ismail and hinted that it would be advisable to agree because the UN Security Council also had its sights on a Darfur inquiry. If there was already an African panel, that might be forestalled.

Bashir rebuffed the AU and set up his own commission instead. It was, inevitably, a complete whitewash. Its report, released in January 2005, was so unbalanced that even some of its own commissioners were furious. The report concluded that crimes had been committed by all sides, and more effort was needed to bring the perpetrators to court. Equivalence was presumed where none existed. No one was named, no government culpability was admitted and not one suspected perpetrator of the war crimes in Darfur was brought to justice.

Bashir grossly misjudged the level of international outrage, especially in America. The US had not been prepared to do much to help the African Union beyond releasing a couple of planes to transport AU troops, and then only for a few days. But Washington was generous with words, more than ready to condemn human rights violations in very strong terms. In response to a Congressional Resolution passed on 24 June 2004 and describing Darfur as 'genocide', the US State Department compiled a report of its own based on research among refugees in Chad. Secretary of State Colin Powell catalogued the horrors in written evidence to the Senate Foreign Relations Committee on

9 September, and noted that 'despite having been put on notice multiple times, Khartoum has failed to stop the violence'.[2] He said that 'genocide has been committed in Darfur and that the government of Sudan and the Jingaweit bear responsibility – and genocide may still be occurring.' It was a historic, but problematic, finding. The key legal issue in determining genocide is intent. The facts on the ground are not proof enough. What matters is what in the mind of the perpetrator. Does he or she intend 'to destroy, in whole or part, a national, ethnical, racial or religious group'?[3] The International Criminal Tribunal for Rwanda found that the men it was prosecuting refused, unsurprisingly, to confess. Bad things happen in war, they said. Musa Hilal echoes that defence, saying, 'There is death in war.'[4]

The Rwanda Tribunal rejected this argument. It reasoned that it was possible to deduce one person's genocidal intent from the general context of other acts 'systematically' directed against the same group. On this basis, it found the mayor of a small Rwandese town, Jean-Paul Akayesu, guilty of genocide. It was first conviction ever for genocide by any court.

At the ICTR, official directives instructing massacre helped clinch the case for genocidal intent. In the case of Darfur, the US State Department inferred both official policy and personal intent from the facts on the ground. Indicating a degree of unease, perhaps, Powell followed his historic determination that genocide was being committed with the caveat that 'No new action is dictated by this determination.... Let us not be too preoccupied with this designation.' It is true that the Genocide Convention does not specify any particular course of action to stop a genocide; it does not, as has been claimed, require the UN to mount a Chapter VII military intervention. It demands only that suspects be prosecuted and, if convicted, punished. Khartoum had signed the Genocide Convention just ten months earlier, and now saw this legalistic quibbling as proof that even an international covenant like the Genocide Convention was just

a piece of paper. The following week, at American behest, the
UN Security Council established the International Commission
of Inquiry on Darfur.

The ICID worked fast and finished its report in little more than
three months. Published on 25 January 2005, it confirmed, in
detail, the pattern of abuses described by the State Department.
It found no evidence of genocidal intent 'as far as the central
Government authorities are concerned'. Attacking, killing and
forcibly displacing civilians did not 'generally' indicate intent
to annihilate that group. In Darfur, the report said, 'it would
seem that those who planned and organized attacks on villages
pursued the intent to drive the victims from their homes, primarily for the purposes of counter-insurgency warfare'.[5] At the
same time, however, the report said that *individuals* – including
government officials – may have possessed genocidal intent. This
was 'a determination that only a competent court can make on
a case by case basis'. It proposed prosecution in an international
court and submitted a sealed list of fifty-one individuals for
criminal investigation. Ten were high-ranking members of the
central government. Seventeen were local government officials,
fourteen *Janjawiid* members and three officers of foreign armies.
Seven were rebel commanders.

Three days before its official release, the ICID report was passed
to Khartoum, which leaked the 'no genocide' finding, ignoring
the corollary that 'International offences such as the crimes against
humanity and war crimes that have been committed in Darfur
may be no less serious and heinous than genocide.'

Khartoum's war, meanwhile, has entered a new phase. Having
declared 'total victory' in February 2004, President Bashir presided
over a *Janjawiid* parade in Nyala on 19 May. He watched proudly
as the horsemen rode past him, shouting and brandishing their
weapons. 'We want all the displaced and the refugees to return
to their homeland', he told the crowd. 'We want the farmers to
return to their areas. We want you to cultivate your farms, and

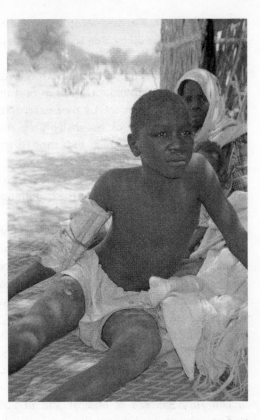

Hussein Dafa'alla

we will provide security and safety... The federal government, the army, the police, the security, the Popular Defence Forces, will all be at the service of the people of Darfur.' For Bashir, peace is subjugation. Massacre and burning largely complete, the government now wields more insidious weapons, camouflaged as measures to provide development and security. Bashir's ministers are manipulating the tribal power structure, putting their own nominees in positions of authority over people and land – and in so doing reducing once self-governing communities to dis-possessed underclasses. Displacement and terror are leaving people who were once self-reliant abjectly dependent on foreign charity and governmental diktat. For Darfurians these actions are indeed 'no less heinous than genocide'.

The serial war criminals at the heart of Sudan's present government once sought absolute control in pursuit of an Islamic state. Now they seek power for its own sake. Today, as yesterday, the people they perceive to be challenging that power count for nothing. They can be subjugated, shot or starved without compunction. If local allies have different axes to grind, they are free to grind them, no matter how much blood they shed. Mass killing has become so routine that it no longer needs conspiracy or deliberation. It is simply how the security elite does business. It is ingrained intent, atrocity by force of habit. The government and Janjawiid are doing more than destroying groups, whether in whole or in part. They are destroying the very soul of Darfur, turning neighbours against each other and dismembering, limb by limb, a society that once thrived in diversity. The shock waves of this crime, if not reversed, will blight the lives of future generations, long outlasting the bloodshed, hunger and grief of today. For many, the past is already a different country – and one they fear they may never recover.

'We did not know the word Janjawiid when we were young', Sheikh Heri Rahman of Muzbat said in 2005, two years short of his eightieth birthday.

> The Arabs came here looking for pasture, and when the grass
> was finished they went back. They used up our grass, but they
> took good care of the gardens and the people. There were
> no robberies, no thieves, no revolution. No one thought of
> domination; everyone was safe. We were afraid only of lions and
> hyenas. Now there is nothing but trouble, all over Sudan. There
> is no government, no control. Look around you. What do you
> see? No women, only armed men. We no longer recognize it,
> this land of ours.

Chronology

c. 1630   Foundation of the Fur Sultanate.

1787   Dar Fur conquers Kordofan.

1821   Egyptian conquest of the Sudanese Nile.

1874   Overthrow of the Fur Sultanate.

1884   Mahdists take control of Dar Fur.

1898   Defeat of the Mahdists and restoration of the Fur Sultanate.

1913   Drought and 'Julu' famine.

1916   Overthrow of Sultan Ali Dinar and incorporation of Darfur into Sudan.

1923   Incorporation of Dar Masalit into Sudan.

1920–30   Creation of 'Native Administration' system.

1956   Independence of Sudan.

1960   Railway reaches Nyala.

1966   Chadian opposition front FROLINAT founded in Nyala.

1969   Jaafar Nimeiri takes power in Sudan.

1970   Ansar and Muslim Brothers flee Sudan.

1971   Native Administration abolished.

1973   Libya starts smuggling weapons to Chadian opposition through Darfur, beginning of Islamic Legion activities in Chad.

1976	Ansar–Muslim Brothers invasion of Sudan from Libya.
1980	A regional government and elected governor provided for Darfur.
1982	Hissène Habré takes power in Chad.
1984	Drought leading to famine in Darfur.
April 1985	Overthrow of Nimeiri and opening of Darfur–Libya border.
1986	Acheikh Ibn Omer sets up Chadian armed camps in Darfur.
1987–89	First Arab–Fur war; first organization of *Janjawiid*.
June 1989	Omer al Bashir takes power in Khartoum.
December 1990	Idriss Deby takes power in Chad.
1991	Darfur becomes a state within a federal system.
December	SPLA incursion into Darfur.
1994	Darfur divided into three states; Native Administration reintroduced.
March 1995	Nine *amirs* appointed for the Arabs in Western Darfur.
1995–99	Arab–Masalit conflict.
1999	Split in ruling Congress Party.
May 2000	Publication of the *Black Book* detailing marginalization of Darfur.
2001	Organization of armed opposition in Darfur.
2002	Conferences at Nyertete and Kas to try to mediate the conflict.
December	Vice-president Ali Osman warns Darfur not to follow the path of the South.
February 2003	SLA announces its existence and publishes manifesto.
March	JEM announces its existence.
April	Rebels attack al Fasher airport.
May	Rebel attacks on Kutum, Mellit, Tine.
July	*Janjawiid* counteroffensive begins in earnest.
September	Government–SLA ceasefire talks in Abeche, Chad.

January 2004   Major government offensive.

March   UN Coordinator Mukesh Kapila calls Darfur 'the world's worst humanitarian crisis' and makes a comparison to Rwanda.

April   Government–SLA/JEM talks in N'Djamena agree on a ceasefire and disarmament of the *Janjawiid*.

June   US Congress describes Darfur as 'genocide'.

July   UN Security Council gives Khartoum thirty days to disarm the *Janjawiid* and facilitate humanitarian assistance.

August   Government and rebels meet in Abuja, Nigeria.

September   US Secretary of State Colin Powell declares Darfur to be 'genocide'; the UN Security Council sets up an Independent Commission of Inquiry into Darfur.

January 2005   ICID delivers its report. Comprehensive Peace Agreement signed between Sudan government and SPLM in Nairobi, Kenya.

July   Government of Sudan, SLA/M and JEM sign Declaration of Principles in Abuja.

Glossary

Abbala	Camel herders
Amir	'Prince': Arab tribal leader under 1995 local government system
Ansar	Followers of the Mahdi
AU	African Union
Baggara	Cattle herders
CDR	Conseil Démocratique Révolutionnaire, Chadian opposition front
DLF	Darfur Liberation Front, forerunner of SLA
Fursha	Middle-ranking administrative chief in Dar Masalit
Fursan	Horsemen
Hakura	Land grant under the Fur Sultanate
ICID	International Commission of Inquiry into Darfur
Islamic Legion	Libyan-established international brigade for Sahelian countries and Sudan
JEM	Justice and Equality Movement
Masar	Livestock migration route
Murahaliin	Baggara militia
Nazir	Paramount chief, usually of an Arab tribe
NCP	National Congress Party

NDA	National Democratic Alliance, umbrella opposition group
NIF	National Islamic Front
Omda	Middle-ranking administrative chief
PCP	Popular Congress Party
PDF	Popular Defence Forces, government paramilitaries
Qoreish	Tribe of the Prophet Mohamed
Quwait al Salaam	'Peace Forces', government militia
Shartai	Senior chief in the Fur hierarchy
Sheikh	Lowest-ranking administrative chief
SLA	Sudan Liberation Army
SPLA	Sudan People's Liberation Army
Wadi	Seasonal watercourse

Notes

Chapter 1

1. See O'Fahey and Abu Salim 1983.
2. This section draws heavily upon the excellent study of Dor in Musa Abdul-Jalil 1984.
3. The phenomenon of richer farmers in the Jebel Marra investing their wealth in cattle, changing their lifestyle and cultural traits, and 'becoming Baggara [Arabs]' was noted in the 1960s. See Haaland 1969.
4. Different people provide different dates for this fight.
5. The proverb is cited by Musa Abdul-Jalil.
6. See Kapteijns 1985.
7. Kapteijns 1985: 78.
8. The Beni Hussein and Zayadiya Arabs both obtained nazirates.
9. Sudan National Archive, Civsec (1) 64-2-11, 'Economic Development Darfur Province', 1945.
10. Daly 1991: 106-8, 123, 260-61, 347.
11. Doornbos 1988.
12. Interviewed in Legediba, May 1986.

Chapter 2

1. Interviewed in N'Djamena, January 2005.
2. Interviewed in Khartoum, January 2005.

3. Ushari and Baldo 1987.
4. Amnesty International 1989; African Rights 1995; Christian Aid 2001.
5. Undated message from Musa Hilal to 'our government, our people and the leaders of the state', around April 2004.
6. de Waal and Abdelsalam 2004.
7. de Waal 2004.

Chapter 3

1. From Alex de Waal's diary, 6 November 1985.
2. BBC interview with Mukesh Kapila, UN Coordinator for Sudan, March 2004.
3. Emily Wax, 'In Sudan, "a Big Sheik" Roams Free', *Washington Post*, 18 July 2004.
4. Philip Sherwell, 'Tribal Leader Accused over Darfur Says He Was Acting for Government', *Daily Telegraph*, 22 August 2004.
5. Wax, 'In Sudan', n2.
6. Interviewed by Human Rights Watch in Khartoum, September 2004.
7. Confidential information to the authors, April 2004.
8. Details from the Sudan National Archive, Khartoum, file Civsec (1) 66/12/107, *Rizeigat*, 1917–41.
9. Ahmed Al-Bashir 1978: 38.
10. Musa Abdul-Jalil 1988: 15.
11. de Waal and Malik 1986: 33, 38–9.
12. Abdel Kassim Ferseldin, 'Devils in Disguise', unpublished essay, 2004.
13. Ruiz 1987.
14. Sharif Harir 1994.
15. 'MPs Charge Conspiracy in Darfur', *Sudan Times*, 15 January 1989.
16. Burr and Collins 1999: 236.
17. Telephone interview, 9 March 2005.
18. See Sharif Harir 1994 for details.
19. 'The leader says "There is a determination in Sudan to bury reactionarism and sectarianism"', *JANA Bulletin*, 28 October 1990.
20. Interviewed in Abuja, December 2004.
21. The Council of West Darfur State, Law Organizing Native Administration, 1999, Part 1 Section 3. Though passed in 1999, the logic and intent were clear from March 1995. A similar provision was made for the most senior Fur chief, the *Dimangawi* of Zalingei.

22. Interviewed in Khartoum, February 2005.
23. The Masalit Community in Exile, 'Not-Ready-For-Prime-Time Genocide', 1999.
24. Interviewed in Abuja, December 2004.
25. Interview with Ibrahim Yahya in Abuja, December 2004.
26. Ibid.
27. Ibid.
28. Interviews in Abuja and N'Djamena, 2004–5.
29. Interviews with in Darfur and Chad, January 2005.
30. Interview with Tom Suleiman Kossa, then leader of the activists, in N'Djamena, January 2005.
31. Interview with Ibrahim Yahya in Abuja, December 2004.
32. Interview with Mansour Nayer Jumaa in Bahai displaced camp, January 2005.
33. Interview with Mubarak Abakir Musa in Bahai displaced camp, January 2005.
34. Interview with Awadalla Nahar in Bahai displaced camp, January 2005.
35. Interview with Ibrahim Yahya in Abjua, December 2004.
36. Interview with SLA Commander Tayyib Bashar in Abuja, January 2005.
37. For details of this camapign, see the *Memorandum submitted by the Darfur Relief and Documentation Centre* to the UK Parliament, 11 January 2005.

Chapter 4

1. Interview in Dar Masalit, March–April 2004.
2. Interviewed in Dar Masalit, April 2004.
3. Interview with Khamis Abakir in Dar Masalit, March 2004.
4. Interviewed in Dar Masalit, March and April 2004.
5. Interviewed in Abuja, December 2004.
6. Interview with Ahmad Abdel Shafi in Abuja, December 2004.
7. Report by Dawud Ibrahim Salih, Muhammad Adam Yahya, Abdel Hafiz Omar Sharief and Osman Abbakorah, representatives of the Masalit Community in Exile, 1999.
8. Interview with Omda Bakhit Dabo Hashem in Bahai refugee camp, January 2005.
9. Sudan Human Rights Organization, *Sudan Government Fails to Insure Stability and Peace in DarFur*, 1 March 2003.
10. Interview with Ahmad Nur in Gorbora, January 2005.
11. Interview with Adam Ali Shogar in Abuja, December 2004.

12. Interview with Sabit Bakhat Hashem in Bahai camp, January 2005.

13. Interviews in Abuja and N'Djamena, December 2004 and January 2005.

14. Some SLA officials say this attack was the first claimed in the name of the DLA, but the claim does not appear to have reached the outside world – most likely because the rebels were not yet equipped with the satellite telephones with which they would, by early 2003, be calling human rights organizations and journalists.

15. Interviews in Abuja, December 2004.

16. Sudan Organization against Torture, press release, 23 August 2002.

17. Interviewed in Khartoum, January 2005.

18. Interview with Jab al Din Hussein in Abuja, December 2004.

19. Fur Diaspora Association, 'Appeal to the International Community to Save the Fur from Genocide', 6 January 2004.

20. Interview with Ahmad Abdel Shafi in Abuja, December 2004.

21. AFP, 'New Rebel Group Seizes West Sudan Town', 26 February 2003.

22. Interviews in Nairobi, April 2005.

23. 'SPLM Position on Developments in Darfur', 20 March 2003.

24. Interviewed in Abuja, December 2004.

25. Interviews in Abuja, Darfur and N'Djamena, December 2004 and January 2005.

26. Interviews with SLA commanders in Darfur, January 2005.

27. Interviews in Abuja, N'Djamena and Dar Zaghawa, December 2004 and January 2005.

28. Interview in Abuja, December 2004.

29. Interviewed in London, April 2005.

30. Telephone interview, February 2005.

31. Report of the International Commission of Inquiry on Darfur to the United Nations Secretary-General, 25 January 2005.

32. Interview with Ahmad Tugod in N'Djamena, January 2005.

33. Interviewed in Abuja, December 2004.

34. *Resolving the Issue of Religion and the State*, www.sudanjem.com.

35. John Ryle, 'Disaster in Darfur', *New York Review of Books*, 15 July 2004.

Chapter 5

1. Scott Anderson, 'How Did Darfur Happen?' *New York Times*, 17 October 2004.

2. Interview with Khamis Abakir.

3. Masalit Community in Exile, press release, 1 April 2003
4. Interviews with rebel commanders in Dar Zaghawa, January 2005.
5. Collins 2004.
6. Interviewed in *The Globe & Mail*, 17 August 2004.
7. Interview with Omda Gamr Musa in Cherkerio, April 2004.
8. Interviews in London, November 2004.
9. Letter from the Office of the Governor, South Darfur State, 2 November 2003, quoted in Human Rights Watch, May 2004.
10. Interview with Khamis Abakir in Dar Masalit, April 2004.
11. Interview with Khamis Yousif Haroun in London, March 2005.
12. 'Ethnic Cleansing in Desert of Death for Black Muslims', *Sunday Telegraph*, 25 April 2004
13. Human Rights Watch, August 2004.
14. Interviewed in Mazare, Chad, 31 March 2004.
15. Interview with Ahmad Abdalla Israel Yahya in Cherkerio, April 2004.
16. Interview with Yousif Mohamed Musa, in Dar Masalit, April 2004.
17. BBC 2, *Sudan's Secret War*, 21 July 1995.
18. Interview with a government defector in Tam, Western Upper Nile, April 2003.
19. According to this document, dated 16 August 2004, the orders were issued at a meeting in the house of Jibriil Abdalla Ali, who in December 2004 visited London as part of a four-man government delegation.
20. Human Rights Watch, July 2004.
21. Interview in Hajjar Bayda, April 2004.
22. Interview in Bahia camp, January 2005.
23. Philip Cox, *Channel 4 News*, February 2004.
24. Interview with Imam Izhaq Abdalla Adam Saber in Cherkerio, Chad, April 2004.
25. ICID 2005.
26. Darfur Association of Canada (Ontario Branch), 'Repatriation of Refugees before the Solution of Problem is a Crime', 15 March 2004.
27. *New York Times*, 18 July 2004.
28. 'Villagers Put Their Lives on the Line to Tell of Atrocities by Sudanese Militia', *The Scotsman*, 25 May 2004.
29. *A Briefing Paper on the Darfur Crisis: Ethnic Cleansing*, Khartoum, 25 March 2004.
30. *Washington Post*, July 2004.
31. Interview in Muzbat, January 2005.
32. Darfur Association of Canada (Branch of Ontario), *Repatriation of Refugees*

before the Solution of Problem is a Crime, 15 March 2004

33. Interview with Omar Angabo in Abuja, December 2004.
34. Interview with a survivor in Cherkerio, April 2004.
35. Interviews in Darfur, March 2004, and Abuja, December 2004.
36. Amnesty International, September 2004.
37. UN Commission of Inquiry Report, 25 January 2005.
38. Human Rights Watch, May 2004.
39. Jan Egeland, UN Under-Secretary for Humanitarian Affairs, cited by the UN News Center, 18 February 2005.
40. Testimony by Roger Winter, assistant director of USAID, to the US Committee on International Relations, 6 May 2004.
41. Amnesty International, January 2005.
42. USAID *Fact Sheet 15, Darfur-Humanitarian Emergency*, 23 July 2004.
43. *Financial Times*, 16 December 2004.
44. Keen 1994.
45. de Waal 1989.
46. Interviewed in *el Da'ien*, December 1986.
47. Nicholas D. Kristof, 'The West Stands by While Genocide Unfolds', *New York Times*, 1 June 2004.
48. Reuters, 'Annan Assures Darfur Displaced of No Forced Return', 1 July 2004.
49. *Al Sahafa*, July 2004.
50. Power 2004.
51. Amnesty International, July 2003.
52. Interviews in Dar Masalit, March–April 2004.
53. Amnesty International, June 2004.
54. Amnesty International, *Urgent Action*, 10 May 2004.
55. 'Villagers Put Their Lives on the Line'.
56. Arab Alliance Political Committee, 'Report on the Visit of the Political Committee of the Arab Alliance to Buram, Tulus, Riheid el-Birdi and 'Id al-Fursan', 15 November 2003.

Chapter 6

1. SOAT, 'Hamada Village Destroyed', 19 January 2005.
2. Colin L. Powell, 'The Crisis in Darfur', written remarks before the Senate Foreign Relations Committee, Washington DC, 9 September 2004.
3. Convention on the Prevention and Prosecution of the Crime of Genocide, 1948, Article II.

4. Scott Anderson, 'How Did Darfur Happen?' *New York Times*, 17 October 2004
5. ICID 2005: 4. This can be read as arguing that although the *actus reus* of genocide may have taken place, the *mens rea* was defeating the rebellion and not destroying the ethnic groups suspected of supporting the rebellion.

Bibliography

African Rights, *Facing Genocide: The Nuba of Sudan*, London, 1995.

Ahmed Abdel Rahman Al-Bashir, 'Problems of Settlement of Immigrants and Refugees in Sudanese Society', D.Phil. thesis, University of Oxford, 1978.

Amnesty International, *Sudan: Human Rights Violations in the Context of Civil War*, London, 1989.

Amnesty International, 'Empty Promises? Human Rights Violations in Government-controlled Areas', 16 July 2003.

Amnesty International, 'Sudan: Incommunicado Detentions, Unfair Trials, Torture and Ill-treatment – The Hidden Side of the Darfur Conflict', 8 June 2004.

Amnesty International, 'Darfur, Sudan: UN Security Council Must Challenge Human Rights Violations', 2 September 2004.

Amnesty International, 'Sudan: Who Will Answer for the Crimes?' London, 18 January 2005.

Burr, J. Millard, and Robert O. Collins, *Africa's Thirty Years' War: Chad, Libya and the Sudan, 1963–1993*, Westview Press, Boulder CO, 1999.

Christian Aid, 'The Scorched Earth: Oil and War in Sudan', London, March 2001.

Collins, Robert O., 'Disaster in Darfur', *African Geopolitics* 15–16, Summer–Fall, October 2004.

Daly, Martin, *Imperial Sudan: The Anglo-Egyptian Condominium, 1934–56*, Cambridge University Press, Cambridge, 1991.

de Waal, Alex, *Famine that Kills: Darfur, Sudan, 1984–1985*, Oxford University Press, Oxford, 1989.

de Waal, Alex, 'The Politics of Destabilization in the Horn, 1989–2001', in Alex de Waal (ed.), *Islamism and Its Enemies in the Horn of Africa*, Hurst, London, 2004.

de Waal, Alex, and A.H. Abdelsalam, 'Islamism, State Power and Jihad in Sudan', in Alex de Waal (ed.), *Islamism and Its Enemies in the Horn of Africa*, Hurst, London, 2004.

de Waal, Alex, and Malik Mohammed el Amin, 'Survival in Northern Darfur 1985–1986', Save the Children Fund, Nyala, January 1986.

Doornbos, Paul, 'On Becoming Sudanese', in T. Barnett and A. Abdelkarim (eds), *Sudan: State, Capital and Transformation*, Croom Helm, London, 1988.

Haaland, Gunnar 'Economic Determinants in Ethnic Processes', in Frederik Barth (ed.), *Ethnic Groups and Boundaries*, Allen & Unwin, London, 1969.

Human Rights Watch, 'Darfur Destroyed', New York, 9 May 2004.

Human Rights Watch, 'Darfur Documents Confirm Government Policy of Militia Support', New York, 20 July 2004.

Human Rights Watch, 'Sudan: Janjaweed Camps Still Active', New York, 27 August 2004.

ICID (International Commission of Inquiry on Darfur), 'Report to the United Nations Secretary-General, Pursuant to Security Council Resolution 1564 of 18 September 2004', United Nations, Geneva, 25 January 2005.

Kapteijns, Lidwien, *Mahdist Faith and Sudanic Identity: The History of the Sultanate of Masalit*, Kegan Paul, London, 1985.

Keen, David, *The Benefits of Famine: A Political Economy of Famine and Relief in Southwestern Sudan, 1983–1989*, Princeton University Press, Princeton NJ, 1994.

Musa Abdul-Jalil, 'The Dynamics of Ethnic Identification in Northern Darfur, Sudan: A Situational Approach', in *The Sudan: Ethnicity and National Cohesion*, Bayreuth African Studies Series, Bayreuth, 1984.

Musa Abdul-Jalil, 'Some Political Aspects of Zaghawa Migration and Resettlement', in F.N. Ibrahim and H. Ruppert (eds), *Rural–Urban Migration and Identity Change: Case Studies from the Sudan*, Geowissenschaftliche Arbeiten, Bayreuth, 1988.

O'Fahey, Rex S., and M.I. Abu Salim, *Land in Dar Fur: Charters and Documents from the Dar Fur Sultanate*, Cambridge University Press, Cambridge, 1983.

Power, Samantha, 'Dying in Darfur', *The New Yorker*, 30 August 2004.

Ruiz, Hiram, 'When Refugees Won't Go Home: The Dilemma of Chadians in Sudan', US Committee for Refugees, Washington DC, 1987.

Ryle, John, 'Disaster in Darfur', *New York Review of Books*, 12 August 2004.

Sharif Harir, '"Arab Belt" versus "African Belt," Ethno-Political Conflict in Dar Fur and the Regional Cultural Factors, in Sharif Harir and Terje Tvedt (eds), *Short-cut to Decay: The Case of the Sudan*, Nordiska Afrikainstitutet, Uppsala, 1994.

Ushari, Mahmud, and Suleyman Baldo, *El Diein Massacre and Slavery in the Sudan*, Khartoum, 1987.

Index